Sigmund Freud

For
Anna, Lara and Ben

Pocket BIOGRAPHIES

Sigmund Freud

STEPHEN WILSON

SUTTON PUBLISHING

First published in 1997 by
Sutton Publishing Limited · Phoenix Mill
Thrupp · Stroud · Gloucestershire · GL5 2BU

British Library Cataloguing in Publication Data
A catalogue record for this book is available from the British
Library.

ISBN 0-7509-1530-7

™ ALAN SUTTON™ and SUTTON™ are the
trade marks of Sutton Publishing Limited

Typeset in 13/18 pt Perpetua.
Typesetting and origination by
Sutton Publishing Limited.
Printed in Great Britain by
The Guernsey Press Company Limited
Guernsey, Channel Islands.

CONTENTS

ACKNOWLEDGEMENTS

My main sources have been the biographies of Ernest Jones and Peter Gay. I am grateful for the hospitality of the Freud Museum, London, and especially to Michael Molnar, Research Director, for his micro-biography. Thanks are also due to Connie Webber, Dov-Ber Kerler, Judith Olszowy and the Czech Centre for helpful information. I am grateful for the encouragement of my friend and colleague, Anthony Storr, my editor, Christine Nicholls, and *editor extraordinaria*, Katherine Wilson.

CHRONOLOGY

6 May 1856	Sigmund Freud born, Freiberg, N. Moravia
1860	Family moves to Vienna
1873	Enters University of Vienna
1876	Enters Brücke's Institute of Physiology
1877	Publishes paper on *Petromyzon*
1879	Translates John Stuart Mill (vol. 12 of his *Collected Works* for the German edition, edited by Theodor Gomperz) during military service
1881	Qualifies MD
1882	Engaged to Martha Bernays
1883	Enters Meynert's psychiatric clinic
1885	Visits Charcot at Salpêtrière
13 Sept. 1886	Marries Martha Bernays
1887	Daughter Mathilde born
1889	Son Martin born
1890	Commences correspondence with Fliess
1891	Son Oliver born; publishes *On Aphasia*
1892	Son Ernst born
1893	Daughter Sophie born
1895	Daughter Anna born; publishes *Studies on Hysteria*, with Breuer
1896	Father dies
1897	Doubts 'seduction theory'

Chronology

1900	Publishes *Interpretation of Dreams*
1902	Title Professor Extraordinarius conferred; founds 'Wednesday Psychological Society', later known as Vienna Psychoanalytic Society
1905	*Three Essays on the Theory of Sexuality*
1906	Correspondence with Jung commences
1909	Honorary Doctorate, Clark University, USA
1910	Founds *Zentralblatt für Psychoanalyse*
1912	Adler and Stekel resign from Vienna Society
1913	End of relationship with Jung
1918	Commences analysing daughter Anna
1919	Son Martin returns after war
1920	Daughter Sophie dies
1923	Onset of jaw cancer; publishes *Ego and Id*; grandson Heinele dies
1924	Granted Freedom of the City of Vienna
1925	Breuer dies; Abraham dies
1926	Reik prosecution; Einstein visits
1929	Ferenczi withdraws
1930	Awarded Goethe Prize; mother dies
1933	Ferenczi dies; Freud's books burnt in Berlin
1936	Elected corresponding member of Royal Society
1938	Flees from Nazi Vienna; publishes *Moses and Monotheism* in London
23 Sept. 1939	Recurrence of cancer; death in London

ONE

RELUCTANT REFUGEE

I can most highly recommend the Gestapo to everyone[1]

In March 1938, the Nazi annexation of Austria unleashed a wave of popular anti-Semitism more virulent than any previously seen in Hitler's Germany. People joyously thronged Vienna to welcome Nazi troops, waving flags, singing and raising their arms in 'Sieg Heil' salutes. Priests celebrated the Führer's accomplishments and flew swastika flags from church steeples; while at the same time elderly Jews were being publicly humiliated, Jewish shops pillaged, Jewish children punched and kicked in the streets, Jewish families terrorised, beaten and murdered in their homes. The anti-Nazi Social Democratic lawyer Hugo Sperber was jack-booted to death, and SA brown-shirts – Hitler's uniformed murderous thugs – killed engineer Isidor Pollack in the same way, while conducting a so-called house search. He had been the director of Pulverfabrik Skoda-Werke-Wetzlera, a chemical factory.

When a similar gang broke into Berggasse 19, the home of Sigmund Freud and his family, an extraordinary scene unfolded. Mrs Freud, finding two or three of the men in her dining room, responded with automatic courtesy and invited the sentry at the door to place his rifle in the umbrella stand and be seated. Fetching the household money, she placed it on the table, as if serving a meal, and encouraged the 'gentlemen' to help themselves. Freud's daughter Anna then escorted the intruders to the safe in another room and opened it. At this point the 82-year-old Freud, frail with cancer, and having been aroused by the disturbance, appeared in the doorway. 'He had a way of frowning with blazing eyes that any Old Testament prophet might have envied,' Ernest Jones, his authorised biographer, tells us, 'and the effect produced by his lowering mien completed the visitors' discomfiture. Saying they would call another day, they hastily took their departure.'[2]

Since the onset of jaw cancer in 1923, Freud had endured multiple operations and prolonged pain, yet he maintained a prodigious capacity for work, a sense of humour undulled by the prosthesis that clicked and rattled in his face, and an indomitable pride. It was not in his nature to surrender. He wanted to be near his surgeon, Hans Pichler, and considered himself too old to move. When an emissary from Switzerland arrived bearing $10,000 raised by Carl Gustav Jung, the erstwhile 'crown prince' of psychoanalysis, with whom Freud had fallen out twenty-five years earlier, he sent him packing with a wave of his hand – 'I refuse to be beholden to my enemies.'[3]

Even after his son Martin was arrested for questioning, on the same day as the events described above, he continued to offer his would-be rescuers all sorts of reasons why he should remain where he was, finally declaring that he could not leave his native land since it would be like a soldier deserting his post. Hindsight shows us the pity of his protests – there was no hope for the Jews of Vienna. Four of Freud's sisters, who had to stay behind, were to perish in concentration camps along with most of the 60,000 other Jews then living in Austria.

In fact, on 13 March, the board of the Vienna Psychoanalytic Society had recommended immediate emigration to all its members, with the intention of reconvening wherever Freud managed to find a home. But it was only the following week, after the Gestapo took Anna and held her all day in their headquarters at the Hotel Metropole, that Freud finally bowed to the inevitable.

Although the German government wanted to expel Jews, by 1938 it had made it virtually impossible for them to transfer assets abroad. Since no country was keen on admitting large numbers of impoverished refugees, millions were trapped as Hitler extended his control over Europe. But Freud had an international reputation, had been honoured by the Royal Society in England two years previously, and some of his friends had wealth and influence.

The American ambassador in Paris, W.C. Bullitt, impressed on his German counterpart the importance of treating Freud well. At the same time he cabled President Roosevelt, asking him to intervene on Freud's behalf. Roosevelt instructed his chargé d'affaires in Vienna to do all he could. The unlikely figure of Mussolini is said to have taken steps to secure Freud's welfare. Princess Marie Bonaparte, connected to the royal houses of both

Greece and Denmark, was especially close to Freud, having sought help from him in the 1920s, and subsequently become committed to the psycho-analytic movement. When permission to leave was ultimately granted, she was in Vienna and able to advance the necessary *Reichsfluchtsteuer*, the money demanded by the Nazi authorities before they would grant an exit permit. Meanwhile, Ernest Jones had been able to persuade the British Home Secretary, Sir Samuel Hoare, to grant generous permission for Freud and his associates to live and work in the United Kingdom. Freud left Vienna on 4 June, but not before his bank account had been confiscated, his publications burned and, in a typical display of totalitarian absurdity, he had been made to sign a document confirming that he had been well treated. It was then that he asked the Nazi commissar if he might add a sentence – 'I can most highly recommend the Gestapo to everyone.'

Between 1933 and 1939 Britain admitted 50,000 Jewish refugees and gave them a relatively hospitable reception, but none could have been warmer than Freud's. He was overwhelmed by kindness, messages of support from strangers, visits from famous people and gifts of antiquities for his collection. Flowers and letters (some simply addressed to Dr Freud, London) arrived continually at the house in Elsworthy Road, which his son Ernst had rented. Writing to his brother Alexander, who had reached safety in Switzerland, Freud waxed lyrical – 'England is a blessed, a happy land, inhabited by kindly, hospitable people; that at least is the impression of the first weeks.'[4] He had arrived just in time and was right to add the rider, for within a month the Home Secretary was reporting to the Cabinet that while he was anxious to do his best, 'there was a good deal of feeling growing up in this country – a feeling which was reflected in Parliament – against the admission of Jews to British territory'.[5]

But Freud felt free in London, free to express his iconoclastic ideas concerning the nature of religion without fear that it would result in the outlawing of psychoanalysis. He never allowed himself to be inhibited by the prospect of offending fellow Jews, and no longer had to be concerned about the reaction of the Catholic Church. He set to work completing the final section of *Moses and Monotheism*, a book he had originally styled an 'historical novel' but increasingly, in the face of hostile criticism, urged as scientific truth. Few people agreed with him then, and almost nobody would now.

Freud's speculations on the origin of religion had already been outlined in *Totem and Taboo*. Just as he saw neurotic symptoms in individuals arising out of stifled incestuous desires, so he thought the irrational beliefs and cherished rituals of religion were a kind of illness, a collective obsessional neurosis. However, there was a difference. Whereas in individuals patricidal wishes and incestuous desires were normally restricted to fantasy, in the history of mankind they were events which had actually taken place. Their consequences were etched into the minds of future generations as part of an unconscious evolutionary inheritance.

Primitive man lived in small hordes, each under the domination of a powerful male. All the females, over whom he exercised sexual dominion, were his property. If his sons aroused his jealousy they were killed, castrated or driven out. The expelled brothers united to murder and then cannibalise their oppressive father. Realising the futility of internecine strife and bound together by the memory of their corporate deed, the brothers eventually instituted a new kind of social contract characterised by renunciation of instinct, prohibition of incestuous marriage, recognition of mutual obligations and the introduction of holy institutions.

What did all this have to do with Moses? According to Freud he was not a Hebrew (or Midianite) child found by Pharaoh's daughter in the bulrushes (she would say that!), but a true son of Egypt who grew up adhering to the monotheistic religion of Akhenaten. In about 1350 BC, when his religion was suppressed, Moses turned to a foreign tribe dwelling at the border and tried to realise his ideals in them. He chose them as his people and quit his homeland, imposing on them an even harsher set of restrictions than his religion had hitherto demanded. In doing so he evoked the archaic memory of the primal horde, placing himself in the role of dominant male (or God) – and suffered a corresponding fate. Unconscious awareness of this terrible act gained later expression in a pervasive sense of guilt, giving rise to ever stricter religious prohibitions. Eventually a new religion arose offering redemption from the 'original sin' through sacrifice of a victim – this religion was Christianity.

Freud stubbornly insisted on the truth of his

account, holding it an essential plank in the argument long after biologists had rejected the possibility that acquired characteristics (such as memories) could be inherited. There is no way that a modern understanding of genetics can be squared with Freud's position that men have always known (independently of education and trans-generational communication) that they once possessed a primal father and killed him.

Nonetheless, looked at from the point of view of modern *cultural* analysis, it is undeniably true that the basic elements in Freud's account are perpetuated in the central myths of Western Judaeo-Christian civilisation. Myths in this sense are not trivial fairy stories, but important narratives upon which a social order is constructed and maintained. Freud's analysis applies not (as he thought) to the history of happenings but rather to the prehistory of sacred stories.

The English version of *Moses* was published shortly after Freud's eighty-third birthday, and managed to scandalise Jews and Christians alike. In a final stroke the unregenerate atheist had deprived Jews of a hero, construed their religion as a guilt-ridden obsessional disease, and reduced Christianity to little more than a delusional nostrum – a way of transferring the blame on to the unredeemed.

Freud had only four more months. He had always been reluctant to take pain-killers, preferring 'to think in torment than not to be able to think clearly'.[6] Now, however, the cancer began to eat into his cheek and the base of the bone around his eye; the pain increased and he was unable to sleep. Consenting to the occasional aspirin he soldiered on, somehow continuing with his analytic work until the end of July. But by September he had reached a state of extreme exhaustion and, calling his doctor to him, said, 'My dear Schur, you remember our first talk. You promised me then you would help me when I could no longer carry on. It is only torture now and no longer has any sense.'[7] Schur administered a third of a grain of morphine, and Freud died on 23 September 1939. He had ceased to be a person and had become, in the words of the poet W.H. Auden, 'a whole climate of opinion'.[8]

BOYHOOD

*I have found that people who know that they are preferred
or favoured by their mother give evidence in their lives of a
peculiar self-reliance and an unshakeable optimism which
often seem like heroic attributes and bring actual success
to their possessors*[1]

Příbor is a small town in the Czech Republic
situated about 130 miles east of Prague, not far
from the Polish border. Formerly known as
Freiberg, most of the population were German-
speaking subjects of the Habsburg/Austro-
Hungarian Empire until its dissolution in 1918. It
was there on 6 May 1856, in a room above a
blacksmith's forge, that Sigismund Freud was born.
As is customary among Jews, the boy was also given
a Hebrew name, Schlomo, after his paternal
grandfather and King Solomon.

Freud was the first son of Amalia (née
Nathansohn), a vivacious 21-year-old Viennese who,

like her husband Jacob, originated from Galicia. Jacob, an unprosperous wool merchant, was twenty years older than his third wife, of milder temperament, and had two grown sons from his first marriage – Emanuel and Philipp, who lived nearby. Emanuel's children, Pauline and John, were to become playmates for the infant Freud. His nephew (ally, opponent and 'partner in crime') was a year older than himself, his half-brothers more or less the same age as his mother, and his father old enough to be a grandparent. Little wonder that the unmasking of hidden truths behind contradictory appearances became a recurrent theme in his future thinking.

Although Freud's father was reared in an orthodox Jewish environment, like many of his generation he had rejected the Hasidic religious practices of his forebears. His marriage to Amalia was solemnised in a Reform ceremony, he did not attend synagogue and allowed his little boy to be taken to church by a devout Roman Catholic nursemaid. Yet he continued to read the Bible at home in Hebrew, to study the Talmud, and to celebrate the passover Seder service, which he could recite by heart. Freud later claimed, with more than a hint of reproach, that he had grown up in complete ignorance of everything that concerned Judaism. Nonetheless, following an early flirtation with German nationalism, he always identified himself as a Jew. If his father had been disinclined to hand on Jewish tradition, then his schoolteacher Samuel Hammerschlag, who emphasised the progressive relevance of the Old Testament to contemporary liberal values, was a source of inspiration to the adolescent boy.

In old age Freud recalled his happy childhood in the bucolic surroundings of Freiberg with a depth of feeling that could scarcely be doubted. Yet it was precisely the intensity of such memories which in 1899 he made the subject of a controversial paper entitled 'Screen Memories'.[2] Here he argues that early memories may be preserved not because they are themselves particularly significant, but because they are linked by chance associations to *later* events which carry a strong emotional charge. Just as he came to think of dreams as representing the disguised fulfilment of unacceptable wishes, so he suggested that apparently unremarkable memories could derive their intensity and importance from later experiences to which they unconsciously alluded. They acted as 'screen memories', disguising wishes that were unacceptable to the conscious mind under the cloak of innocent childhood activity.

Space does not permit a detailed recapitulation of Freud's argument, but the following account of an early memory (said to be that of a patient) is almost certainly autobiographical: 'a rectangular, rather steeply sloping piece of meadow-land, green and thickly grown; in the green there are a great number of yellow flowers – evidently common dandelions. At the top of the meadow there is a cottage and in front of the cottage door two women are standing chatting busily, a peasant woman with a handkerchief on her head and a children's nurse.'[3] A small boy is collecting flowers together with his cousins (actually Freud's nephew and niece). The girl has the best bunch but the two boys snatch it away from her. She bursts into tears and is given black bread in consolation. Later the boys too are given bread by the women.

In the memory the yellow of the flowers has an incandescent quality, and the taste of the bread is deliciously real, like a hallucination. It might seem to hark back to an idyllic childhood and require no further explanation, but Freud saw its occurrence as problematic. Why was this particular and apparently commonplace episode preserved with such intensity? And why did the recurrent memory only begin in later life? In short, Freud concluded it was because he had revisited the same area as a teenager and fallen in love with Gisela Fluss, a girl he had known there in childhood. She was wearing a yellow dress. The scene in which he took yellow flowers from his little niece was a disguised fulfilment of his wish to deflower the older girl, and gained its force from the young man's suppressed sexual imagination.

Effectively Freud was an only child at birth, doted on by mother and nanny alike, but it was not long before his status in the family was challenged by the arrival of siblings. A younger brother Julius was born after eighteen months whom Freud greeted 'with adverse wishes and genuine childhood jealousy'. When Julius died seven months later, Freud was left with a deeply implanted sense of guilt. In 1858 his sister Anna was born, and during his mother's confinement his beloved nursemaid was caught thieving by his half-brother Philipp, arrested and sent to prison.

Her disappearance at the same time as his mother generated a desperate sense of loss in the little boy.

Although the 1848 revolution brought increased freedom and political emancipation to millions across Europe, it also coincided with the growth of national movements within the Austro-Hungarian Empire. With the rise of Czech nationalism during the second half of the century and the growth of a Czech bourgeoisie, the position of Jewish traders in the agrarian economy came under threat. Anti-Jewish boycotts and local co-operatives designed to avoid Jewish middlemen were formed. In response, a significant movement of the Jewish population to the capital city took place.

Jacob Freud was not alone in transferring his family to Leopoldstadt, Vienna – thousands of others flocked there. When the family arrived in 1860 there were four of them, but by the time Freud reached the age of ten he had another five siblings – Rosa, Marie, Adolfine, Pauline and Alexander. These were impoverished years, spent crowded together in less than satisfactory accommodation, until in 1885 they eventually moved to a larger flat. Even then his parents and five siblings shared three bedrooms, but the 'golden boy' had a self-contained room of his own, with a window looking out on to the street, bookshelves, chair, writing desk and an oil lamp – the others had to make do with candles. It was in this 'cabinet' that Freud lived until the end of his university days.

He had a brilliant career at school, entering the gymnasium (grammar school) a year early and coming top of his class for six of the last eight years. He read widely outside the official syllabus and mastered Latin, Greek, French, English and Italian as well as becoming an elegant stylist in German. Together with his bosom friend Eduard Silberstein Freud formed a learned society named 'Academia Cartellane'. It had two members. They taught themselves Spanish and were much taken by Cervantes' tale 'The Dogs' Colloquy', in which two dogs engage in a philosophical dialogue. The boys adopted the dogs' names as signatures – Freud was Scipio and Silberstein Berganza.

If Freud's talents and success gained the esteem of his father, it was not reciprocated by the growing boy. Jacob's disqualification from his son's pantheon of heroes was intimately related to his identity as a Jew (and to traditional Diaspora passivity), in a country where anti-Semitism was endemic. One day he told the twelve-year-old boy that a Gentile had knocked off his new fur cap and shouted at him 'Jew, get off the pavement!' When asked about his response Freud's father calmly replied, 'I stepped into the gutter and picked up my cap.'[4] Freud contrasted his father's behaviour unfavourably with that of Hamilcar, the Carthaginian general who made his small son Hannibal swear eternal hatred of the Romans. He also admired Napoleon's Jewish general, Marshal Masséna. Throughout his life Freud identified with military heroes. Even in 1938 as an elderly refugee crossing the English Channel he managed to dream that he was William the Conqueror landing at Pevensey.

In adolescence he was a typical overbearing big brother. He helped his sisters with their studies, but attempted to censor their reading matter, forbidding Balzac and Dumas, issued pompous homilies on their behaviour and complained about the noise from their piano practice. The piano was of course removed. At the age of seventeen he graduated *summa cum laude* – he must have been insufferable.

Despite the continued existence of cultural anti-

Semitism, Vienna in the 1860s when Freud was growing up was a window of political liberalism during which virtually every legal restraint against Jews was removed. The principle that citizens of all persuasions enjoy equal rights was espoused by the authorities and eagerly embraced by young assimilated Jews. They could now aspire to full civic participation and membership of the professions. It was the period during which, as Freud noted in *The Interpretation of Dreams*, 'every industrious Jewish schoolboy carried a minister's portfolio in his satchel'.[5] Freud was no exception; his early thoughts led him towards a career in law but his natural inclination pointed in the direction of medical science. Accordingly he entered the Medical Faculty of Vienna University in autumn 1873, with no special enthusiasm for an eventual career in clinical practice.

He was only seventeen and, in addition to the regular study of anatomy and physiology, continued to read widely. He attended optional courses in philosophy run by Franz Brentano, a lapsed Catholic priest who had been unable to subscribe to the Vatican's doctrine of papal infallibility. He also did extra courses in physics and zoology, making the study of marine animals his special interest. In March 1876 his first research project took him to an experimental marine biology station in Trieste in search of the gonads of the mature eel. Nobody, save a Polish researcher named Simone de Syrski, had ever seen them, since adults migrated before the mating period. His findings needed to be confirmed. Freud dissected four hundred specimens and found the elusive testicular tissue in many of them – but his results were equivocal and did not satisfy him.

However, shortly after returning from Trieste Freud was accepted as a research student in Ernst Brücke's famous Institute of Physiology, where (concurrently and somewhat at the expense of his clinical studies) he continued to research neuro-anatomical problems for the next six years. He had found his vocation and was content to model himself on the great scientists he was working alongside. Brücke suggested a project looking into the structure of cells in the spinal cord of the Petromyzon (a primitive fish), and his enthusiastic young acolyte soon devised an improved formula for preparing the necessary microscope slides. The wider purpose was to establish whether lower vertebrates possessed the same kind of nerve cells as higher ones and thus to investigate evolutionary continuity.

After two years of painstaking work, Freud was able to confirm that the fish did indeed possess similar nerve cells to those found in higher animals. This was important work in its time, followed up by a parallel investigation into the nervous tissue of the crayfish. By 1881, when Freud belatedly qualified as a physician, he had added to his research credentials with the invention of a new gold chloride method for staining nervous tissue. He had never seen himself as a practising doctor and, at this stage, looked set for a career in the higher echelons of academic physiology.

THREE

DISCOVERY

In my last severe depression I took coca again and a small dose lifted me to the heights in a wonderful fashion. I am just now busy collecting the literature for a song of praise to this magical substance[1]

Freud had the intellectual equipment, the application and the ambition necessary for success in the field of medical science, but he did not have the money. Although he continued to work as a demonstrator in the Physiological Institute, he was paid little and continued to rely on handouts which his elderly father could ill afford. Even to maintain a modest standard of living he needed extra financial assistance, which was increasingly supplied by a benevolent senior colleague, Josef Breuer. Breuer was a wealthy, well-established physician and outstanding physiologist who supplemented Freud's allowance with regular loans. Their future collaboration in the study of hysteria (illness which defies biological explanation) was to catalyse the development of psychoanalysis. However, despite Breuer's generous help Freud's economic situation was obviously untenable.

He might have continued to turn a blind eye to the sheer impracticality of his chosen career, were it not for the fact that in April 1882 he met, fell in love with and two months later became engaged to marry Martha Bernays. Five years his junior, Martha was pale and petite with a keen intelligence, and, Freud felt, a character imbued with goodness and understanding. She came from a family distinguished in Jewish culture and intellectual pursuits. Her grandfather had been Chief Rabbi of Hamburg and was related to the German-Jewish poet Heine. One uncle was a professor of German in Munich (having renounced his faith), and another taught Latin and Greek at the University of Heidelberg. Her father, who was secretary to a well-known Viennese economist, had died more than two-and-a-half years previously. Since her family was not rich, there was no question but that marriage would create rather than solve economic problems.

When Brücke, as Freud wrote later in his *Autobiographical Study*, 'corrected my father's generous improvidence by strongly advising me, in view of my bad financial position, to abandon my theoretical career',[2] Freud could not fail to see the wisdom of his words. If he was to be in a position to marry, he needed to have an income from private practice. Accordingly, he left the laboratory and took up a position in the General Hospital of Vienna, where for the next three years he was to rotate through its departments in a programme of postgraduate training.

However, far from relinquishing his research ambitions, Freud now transferred them into the clinical field. He was constantly on the lookout for a 'discovery' which would bring him fame and fortune, establish his reputation and secure his livelihood for the future. At the same time he wooed Martha with a curious blend of romantic passion and prosaic realism. During their four-year engagement his emotions fluctuated wildly, and he was unreasonably jealous, sometimes elated and sometimes depressed. Moreover, he suffered from a range of physical conditions which included migraine and mouth infections. The unshakeable optimism supposedly characteristic of a favourite child was often shaken. But he came within a hair's-breadth of making the discovery he so ardently desired.

In April 1884 he read of a German army doctor who had successfully employed cocaine as a means of increasing the energy and endurance of soldiers. He determined to obtain some for himself and try it as a treatment for other conditions – heart disease, nervous exhaustion and morphine addiction. It was little known at that time and the extensive ethical and methodological rules governing modern drug trials did not exist.

Freud took some himself and was immediately impressed with the sense of well-being it engendered, without diminishing his capacity for work. Having read a report in the *Detroit Medical Gazette* concerning its value in the treatment of addictions, his next step was to recommend the substance as a harmless substitute to his friend and colleague, Ernst von Fleischl-Marxow. Fleischl, who had become a morphine addict following repeated therapeutic administrations for intractable neuro-logical pain and was in desperate straits, took to cocaine with enthusiasm and was soon consuming it in large quantities.

Meanwhile Freud continued to extol the virtues of the drug, writing a review essay on the subject, taking it himself and pressing it upon his fiancée, friends, colleagues and patients as a panacea for all ills. He had gone overboard with enthusiasm, writing to Martha when he heard she had lost her appetite, 'Woe to you my Princess, when I come. I will kiss you quite red and feed you 'til you are plump. And if you are forward you shall see who is the stronger, a gentle little girl who doesn't eat enough or a big wild man *who has cocaine in his body*.'[3]

Among the people to whom Freud introduced cocaine was his colleague Carl Koller, a young doctor working in the department of ophthalmology. Freud published his essay in the July issue of the *Centralblatt für Therapie*, concluding it by drawing attention to the possible future uses of the drug as a local anaesthetic. Koller was impressed, thought it likely to be useful in eye operations and two months later tried it out, first on animals and then on his own eyes with complete success. He was quick to publish his findings, thus securing a place in world history as the discoverer of what turned out to be virtually the only medical use for the substance.

Freud had missed his chance, but worse was to follow. Fleischl's temporary improvement on taking cocaine was short lived. Within a week his condition deteriorated, his pain became unbearable and he relapsed into morphine consumption. He now had not one addiction but two, taking cocaine in doses a hundred times larger than Freud used to do. He suffered toxic confusional states in which he became agitated, experiencing severe anxiety and visual hallucinations. Yet Freud continued to advocate the use of cocaine in morphinism, presumably on the basis that (as had been reported by others) it was beneficial in selected cases.

His paper 'On the General Effect of Cocaine', written in the spring of 1885, was published in August and subsequently abstracted in the *Lancet*. By the following year, however, cases of cocaine addiction and intoxication were being reported from all over the world. Freud came under severe criticism for his advocacy of the drug and defended himself by claiming (inaccurately) that he had never advised its use in subcutaneous injections.

Freud evidently preferred to 'forget' his premature assessment of Fleischl's improvement and his rush into overconfident claims for the safety of cocaine. Critics have seized upon this episode as a flaw in Freud's integrity and used it to discredit his later ideas. However, we should be circumspect in attributing blame. Since Fleischl's condition prior to taking cocaine was pitiable and unresponsive to all known medicine, it warranted the consideration of heroic means. Having taken the drug himself in moderate dosage, Freud knew perfectly well that consumption did not inevitably escalate into full-scale addiction, nor was he in a position to regulate the excessive quantities that Fleischl went on to obtain. Toxic effects are dose related rather than linked to any specific route of administration, and the question of whether cocaine produces true physical dependence remains open to doubt. Indeed some modern physicians have advocated a re-exploration of its therapeutic potential.[4]

Despite the unhappy experience with Fleischl, Freud continued to enjoy the support of Brücke and professors Theodor Meynert in the psychiatric clinic and Hermann Nothnagel in general medicine. On their recommendation he was promoted to the coveted rank of *Privatdozent* in autumn 1885. This was a kind of honorary lectureship which gave him a position in the university and carried high prestige with the general public. Achieving it meant that he could enter private practice with a reasonable hope of securing a living.

Psychiatry in Germany and Austria at the end of the nineteenth century was militantly organic in its approach. Great strides had been made by applying the methods of physical science to bodily diseases and the hope was (and still is among many psychiatrists) to find a similar basis for mental disorder. Medical attitudes towards hysteria, an illness supposedly confined to women, involving multiple symptoms lacking a demonstrable cause and resistant to treatment, were characterised by lofty disdain. 'Nervous' patients who thronged the clinics and consulting rooms of physicians, the historian Hannah Decker tells us, 'were usually given large doses of contempt, thinly disguised by treatments of electrical stimulation and prescriptions of vile-tasting medicines like asafoetida'.[5]

But in France the situation was different, and both hysteria and the dubious process of hypnotism had become respectable subjects for medical concern. The great neurologist Jean Martin Charcot had taken an interest in the condition and even more remarkably demonstrated that paralyses could be both induced and relieved through hypnosis. Clearly this suggested that an unconscious 'idea' could give rise to a bodily dysfunction.

Charcot believed that the predisposition to hysteria arose from hereditary brain disease, but that the symptoms were triggered by emotional experiences and were thus amenable to a psychological approach. He also believed that only hysterics were susceptible to hypnotism. However, a rival school in Nancy associated with the name of Hippolyte Bernheim took a different view, maintaining that hypnotism was purely a matter of suggestion and did not depend on pre-existing neuropathology; hence anybody could be hypnotised. If hypnotic states were equivalent to hysterical ones, this undoubtedly implied that they too were purely psychological in origin.

Hysteria remains a controversial subject in modern psychiatry and some would deny its existence altogether, claiming it is no more than a name for medical ignorance. Yet even today, there remain significant numbers of patients who present with 'pseudoneurological' symptoms for which no medical explanation can be found.[6]

Charcot's hospital, the Salpêtrière, had become a

Mecca for visiting neurologists and Freud, disillusioned with the clinical practice he had observed in Vienna, now looked to Charcot for inspiration. Having obtained a travelling scholarship he arranged six months' leave of absence and, after a short visit to Martha and her mother, arrived in Paris in October.

He was not disappointed. Charcot's clinical skill, intellectual acumen and charismatic personality energised Freud every bit as much as the cocaine which he continued to take during his stay in the French capital. He wrote glowing letters to Martha describing his experience – 'that no other human being has ever acted on me in this way I know for certain'. After two months he wrote tentatively to the master enquiring whether he might produce a German translation of his *Lessons* and was overjoyed to receive his consent.

It was Charcot's influence that turned Freud's interest towards psychopathology and throughout his life he was fond of quoting his aphorisms. 'La théorie, c'est bon, mais ça n'empêche pas d'exister. [Theory is fine but it doesn't stop facts from existing.]'[7] was a favourite warning against the uncritical acceptance of received wisdom. Freud hung an engraving of André Brouillet's painting *La Leçon clinique du Dr Charcot* in his consulting room at Berggasse 19, and when his first son was born in 1889 named him Jean Martin in honour of his teacher.

FOUR

The Study of Hysteria

The procedure is laborious and time-consuming for the physician. It presupposes great interest in psychological happenings, but personal concern for the patients as well[1]

Before Freud left for Paris he had been offered the part-time directorship of a new neurological department, to be opened in the Institute for Children's Diseases run by the paediatrician Max Kassowitz. In spring 1886, on returning to Vienna, he took up the post, which he held for many years. Several publications in the field of neurology derive from this period, most notably in 1891 a monograph concerning speech difficulties caused by brain damage – *On Aphasia*. At the same time, he attempted to establish himself in private practice. Neither endeavour was richly remunerative, especially since Breuer had advised him that the best way to build up a reputation was to treat patients free of charge. There were times when he found himself unable to afford the cab fare for a house call. Still, his senior colleagues did refer some paying patients – most came from Breuer, and Nothnagel referred the Portuguese ambassador.

Long engagements were not uncommon in Freud's circle – Fleischl's had been going on for ten years – but since Martha lived in Wandsbek, near Hamburg, she and Freud scarcely had an opportunity to meet. Four years was long enough, and they determined to be married. With the help of a gift from her wealthy aunt Lea Löwbeer, an adequate dowry was at last achieved and the wedding was planned for September. Then, in June, Freud was unexpectedly called for a month's military service, which meant a month's loss of income. Frau Bernays, who had all along been less than enthusiastic about her daughter's future husband, who lacked both money and religion, immediately tried to delay the match.

She wrote to Freud, chastising him for his ill-humour, accusing him of behaving like a spoilt child and demanding that he come to his senses: 'Don't think that I can't imagine how uncomfortable your present life is, but to run a household without the means for it is a *curse*. It is one I have myself borne for many years, so I can judge. I beg and implore you not to do it. Do not let my warning go unheeded, and wait quietly until you have a settled means of existence.'[2]

The two families were in fact already linked by marriage, Martha's brother, Eli, having married Freud's eldest sister, Anna, three years earlier. This could only have rubbed salt into the frustrated couple's wounds, since they were the first to have become engaged. But now there was no holding them back. The military manoeuvres finished on 10 September 1886 and three days later Freud and Martha were married at Wandsbek town hall.

Freud had been adamantly opposed to a religious ceremony, threatening to turn Protestant rather than participate. Ironically it turned out that Austrian law required one, and a quiet Jewish service occurred the following day in Martha's home. The pair honeymooned by the Baltic, returning to Vienna and marital domestic life on 1 October.

Theirs was a traditional lifestyle, Freud devoting himself to professional work while Martha eagerly embraced the role of wife and mother. In October 1887 their first child arrived, a girl named Mathilde after Breuer's kindly wife – 'When we hear the baby laugh we imagine it is the loveliest thing that can happen to us,'[3] Freud later wrote. And in December 1889 Jean Martin was born to add to their happiness. Martha gave birth to four more children in the next five years: Oliver (after Cromwell, another of Freud's heroes), Ernst, Sophie and Anna.

Late in 1896 Martha's unmarried sister, Minna Bernays, joined the household. Following the untimely death of her fiancé she had become a lady's companion, but did not take to the job, preferring to live with her own family. She had a sharp wit, shared Freud's intellectual and literary interests and helped her sister with the children. Freud is sometimes supposed to have been a stern and distant patriarch, but nothing could be further from the truth. Although he worked long hours, to his children he was a cheerful, generous and loving father, whom they had to themselves during the summer vacations. Then he would throw aside professional cares and take them mountain climbing and mushroom hunting, bringing the spoils back for

Martha and 'Tante Minna' to prepare. He was, as his son Martin recalls, 'all laughter and contentment'.[4]

Like all young doctors setting out in practice, Freud soon encountered the limitations of medical science. He was not impressed with the efficacy of current methods, particularly the treatment available to those suffering from psychological problems. The Weir Mitchell 'rest cure', named after the famous American neurologist who invented it, is an example of what was in vogue at the time. Though innocuous sounding, the 'rest cure' was actually a form of torture, involving coerced inactivity. Patients were isolated in bed for six to eight weeks, forbidden to sit up, sew, read or use their hands in any way. At the same time they were overfed and given electric shocks and daily bodily massage. By contrast, the hypnotic technique which Freud brought back from France, which involved overcoming the patient's 'pathological ideas' with the force of the physician's suggestions, seemed the epitome of non-intrusion.

What was foreign to all these methods, however, was the notion that the neuropathic patient might have something to contribute; that his or her experience was in any way relevant to the treatment outcome.

Freud was unusual, but not alone, in thinking it worthwhile to listen to what the patient said. In fact it was Breuer who, in 1882, had first drawn Freud's attention to a case where he had used hypnotism not 'to put ideas into the patient's head', but to help her get them out – to facilitate her own self-expression.

The case was that of Anna O, an intelligent but (according to Breuer) sexually immature 21-year-old girl, now known to have been Martha's friend Bertha Pappenheim. She had been devotedly nursing her dying father until one day she collapsed into a state of mental and physical exhaustion. In addition to a severe nervous cough, occasional muteness, a squint and various other visual disturbances, she developed paralysis of the right arm and neck and suffered a terrifying hallucination of a black snake threatening her father. Her own fingers turned into little snakes. There were also bizarre speech problems; for instance, she could understand when spoken to in German, but often replied in English, and sometimes in French or Italian. She also developed a dual personality. Her 'sick' personality lived exactly 365 days earlier than her 'normal' personality, appearing to re-experience the events of the previous year.

In 1881 her father died, and her hallucinations became more violent during the daytime. However, in the evenings she fell into a quiet trance and began to mumble words. Breuer tried to understand what she was saying, and describing her experiences to him appeared to have a calming effect; but if she failed to do so, the rest of the night was spent in extreme anxiety.

Eventually Breuer decided to induce the hypnotic states himself. Under hypnosis Anna was able to remember how her symptoms began. For example, she revealed that the onset of her squint was an occasion when she had been by her father's side and feeling upset. He had suddenly asked the time. Since she was unable to see her watch without turning her head and revealing her state of distress, she had brought it close to her eyes and squinted at it through her tears. This recollection appeared to relieve the visual disturbance.

Recalling such events was painful, but if the origin of a given symptom could be traced and emotionally re-experienced, it seemed to disappear. Breuer called it the 'Cathartic Method' and Anna O, more graphically, called it 'Chimney Sweeping' and the 'Talking Cure'. It was an extremely time-consuming procedure, since Anna needed to report in reverse chronological order the details of every occurrence of a particular symptom until she reached its putative origin. Her deafness had seven different forms and dealing with just one of those forms, 'not hearing when someone came in', involved Breuer in listening to 108 different instances!

Speculation, both informed and ill-informed, as to the true nature of Bertha Pappenheim's illness, has continued for more than a century. Since it is difficult enough to diagnose such complex conditions when they are actually happening, the chances of ever resolving the issue seem remote. Nonetheless, historical research has revealed Breuer's case report to have been economical with the truth. When her treatment ended in July 1882, she did not merely leave Vienna and travel for a while, as Breuer indicated, but was referred to Dr Robert Binswanger's Swiss sanatorium, Bellevue, at Kreuzlingen. There she stayed for more than a year, continuing to suffer from persistent symptoms and being treated with high doses of chloral and morphine. Ultimately, however, Bertha did recover and went on to become an innovative social worker and feminist. She was the German translator of

Mary Wollstonecraft's famous book, *A Vindication of the Rights of Women*.

Perhaps more remarkable than Bertha Pappenheim's condition, which is paralleled by other cases of hysteria reported at the end of the nineteenth century, was the extraordinary involvement of her physician Josef Breuer. Breuer, a busy doctor, saw her on a daily basis for more than a year, and in the later stages twice daily. He hung upon her every word. When he was absent her symptoms worsened, and would not yield to any locum practitioner, even when the same technique was employed.

On the very evening when Breuer fondly thought he had cured Bertha of all her symptoms, he was, Freud later claimed, called back in an emergency to find her confused and writhing with abdominal cramps, apparently suffering from a phantom pregnancy. Asked what the matter was, she replied, 'Now comes Dr B's child.' According to Ernest Jones, Breuer fled the house in a cold sweat and next day left for Venice with his wife on a second honeymoon.[5] Years later, in 1932, writing to his friend Stefan Zweig, Freud commented that at that moment 'Breuer held the key in his hand', but was unable or unwilling to use it.[6]

The opportunity for emotional expression which Breuer had naively fostered and abruptly terminated was to become the hallmark of psychoanalytic treatment. Where Breuer turned with distaste from his compromising and unsought role as an object in Anna O's fantasies, Freud threw professional caution to the wind and positively embraced such experiences, making them serve as a source of psychological information – a process for which he later coined the term 'transference'.

Freud's early championing of hypnosis had been badly received in Viennese medical circles and, despite Breuer's distinguished reputation, their joint publication in 1895, *Studies on Hysteria*, describing the origin of the new 'Cathartic Method', did no better. Both were agreed that 'Hysterics suffer mainly from reminiscences,'[7] but Freud laid considerable emphasis on the sexual nature of the suppressed memories. Breuer equivocated, preferring, it seems, to distance himself from controversy.

By the time the book was published, their relationship had cooled. Freud's disappointment in Breuer turned to hostility and contempt. It was a classic bite into the feeding hand, and although the bitterness eventually diminished, they never regained their former intimacy. Freud was later to recognise this sad situation as typical of his emotional life.

FIVE

FREUD AND FLIESS

An intimate friend and a hated enemy have always been
indispensable to my emotional life[1]

Insisting on the psychological basis of hysteria, advocating a sexual cause and claiming that men as well as women exhibited the condition were not popular ideas. But Freud's intellectual and professional isolation were as much a product of his own withdrawal as they were of establishment prejudice. Having by 1896 lost two father figures, a rigorous Brücke and an indulgent Breuer, he now turned for companionship to a man of his own generation, the Berlin ear, nose and throat specialist, Wilhelm Fliess.

Ironically it was Breuer who, in 1887, had been the instrument of their first meeting, having recommended Fliess to include Freud's lectures in a study-tour of Vienna. Fliess's attendance indicated that he was no ordinary surgeon. His interests ranged widely in both science and the arts. While still a medical student he had contributed articles to a prestigious Berlin newspaper and reported on important medical congresses. Breuer considered him to be 'one of the richest intellects' he had ever met.[2] He was a brilliant conversationalist and knowledgeable in the fields of mathematics and biology.

In addition he shared much in common with Freud. His father, Jacob Fliess, was a Jewish grain dealer who had moved to Berlin in 1862 and had high ambitions for his son's academic success. At university, Fliess had studied under the distinguished scientists, Hermann Helmholtz, Emil du Bois-Reymond and Rudolf Virchow, who all followed the positivist school of thought which held that an understanding of human functioning must be based on mathematics and natural science, rather than appeal to non-material 'vital' causes. Fliess was also in private practice but, unlike Freud who lacked confidence in his medical knowledge, he was supremely self-assured.

Another trait the two young physicians shared was

a tendency to speculative theorising. Both had been nurtured in scientific backgrounds but both were now engaged in projects that leap-frogged considerably beyond the bounds of scientific respectability. Where Freud was seeking to found a general psycho-biology on notions of instinct and quantities of psychic energy, Fliess was concerned with bio-rhythms and their expression in human life.

Fliess believed that in all living beings there existed female and male rhythms centred on the numbers 28 and 23. These determined a vast array of biological phenomena, including dates of birth, death, illnesses, etc., and were themselves related to the movement of heavenly bodies. He also thought that he had discovered a 'nasal reflex neurosis', linking inflammation of the nasal mucous membranes to dysfunction in other parts of the body, especially the genitals. He erroneously took the effects of cocaine on the brain (absorbed into the bloodstream via the nasal mucosa) to confirm his hypothesis, and believed that by operating on the nose and removing or cauterising certain areas a range of neuralgic problems could be helped.

There can be no doubt that Freud became utterly infatuated with Wilhelm Fliess. He took on board his cranky numerology and subscribed enthusiastically to his outlandish promotion of the nose as a pathogenetic organ. 'Only someone who knows he is in possession of the truth writes as you do,' he worshipfully declared.[3] Not only did he allow Fliess to operate twice on his own nose, but he called him in to advise on the benefits of nasal surgery for his patients. When one of them, Emma Eckstein, developed a severe post-operative haemorrhage due to a piece of iodoform gauze that Fliess had inadvertently failed to remove, Freud exculpated Fliess from all blame and perversely continued to ascribe the bleeding to Emma's 'hysterical' condition.

J.M. Masson, the editor of the Freud–Fliess letters, has made much of this episode in casting doubt on the validity of Freud's later thinking.[4] Doubtless Freud's idealisation of Fliess did blind him to the reality of Emma Eckstein's condition and interfered with his physicianly sympathy, but this has little bearing on the theoretical question as to whether early sexual abuse is a necessary precondition for the development of hysteria – answered by Freud at first in the affirmative and later in the negative.

For ten years, between August 1890 and September 1900, they corresponded regularly. Freud poured his heart out, often more than once a week, confiding not only ideas, plans and professional activities, but intimate details of his own life (which he withheld from Martha) and that of his family. They enjoyed meeting in Vienna and Berlin, but most of all liked to arrange two- or three-day trips away from home, when, free from domestic concerns, they could concentrate on the development of their ideas. It was a mutual admiration society, not unlike the 'Academia Cartellane' of Freud's childhood, whose special meetings were designated 'Congresses'. Fliess was 'the Kepler of biology',[5] and his praise 'nectar and ambrosia' to the hungry Freud.[6]

During this period, although he maintained outward equanimity, Freud's moods swung wildly from elation to depression, just as they had done in the course of his engagement. Sometimes he convinced himself of the value of his discoveries; at other times he was plagued with self-doubt. In addition he was troubled with anxiety symptoms: fear of travelling by rail, dread of dying, shortness of breath and cardiac arhythmias, headaches and recurrent sinusitis. Fliess tried to get him to give up smoking (twenty cigars a day), and frequently prescribed cocaine. Yet out of this turmoil, which the historian Henri Ellenberger has referred to as 'a creative illness',[7] some of Freud's most profound insights arose. Fliess acted as a sounding board for Freud's burgeoning ideas, as he set his analytical mind the task of rectifying itself through introspective scrutiny. This process culminated in 1900 with the publication of *The Interpretation of Dreams,* and the demise of their extraordinary affair.

The reasons for its ending are difficult to fathom and, as in Breuer's case, involve theoretical disputes which seem secondary to the underlying emotional conflict. It would appear that during their last 'Congress' in August 1900, the contradiction between Fliess's numerical determinism and Freud's psychodynamic principles finally struck home. Afterwards there was a definite lull in the correspondence, yet both of them claimed to have enjoyed the meeting,[8] Fliess continued to refer patients and in January 1901 we find Freud addressing him affectionately as 'My Dear One'. It is all the more surprising to suppose that Freud planned (or attempted) murder during their last meeting, as Fliess later alleged.[9] In any event, the row which marked their final separation, concerning the alleged plagiarism of Fliess's ideas on bisexuality by a friend of one of Freud's patients, seems mild by comparison.

Since the theoretical issues with which Freud was grappling remain a matter of current concern, it is worth setting out the story more fully. During the period 1892–6 he had gradually abandoned the use of hypnotism, finding it difficult to induce and being uncertain in its effects. At first he substituted a 'pressure technique', in which the patient was asked to relax on a couch and try to recall anything that seemed relevant to a particular symptom. If nothing came to mind, Freud would press the patient's forehead with his hand and insist that some thoughts would occur. As time went by, he adopted a less interventionist approach, realising that he would learn more by allowing the patient's thoughts to evolve freely.

Freud was impressed by four aspects of the stories which emerged in this way: the ubiquity with which an early sexual experience was recounted, the reluctance on the part of the patient to tell of it, the distress caused while doing so, and the relief brought about afterwards. He concluded that a history of forgotten sexual awakening existed in every case of hysteria and obsessional neurosis. However, he observed that the symptoms of the illness appeared not at the time when the sexual event originally took place, but many years later. He therefore proposed that the 'delayed action' was brought about after puberty by retrospectively investing the dormant memories with an intolerable sexual force which had to be suppressed. This was the 'seduction theory', which, as can be seen, had much in common with the notion of 'screen memories'.

In September 1897, however, in a now famous letter, Freud confessed to Fliess, 'I no longer believe in my *neurotica*',[10] by which he meant his theory of the neuroses. Once again his treatments had been unsatisfactory and had often been broken off prematurely. But most of all he realised that if sexual abuse was an essential but insufficient condition for the development of hysteria, the sheer prevalence of the disorder would indicate that perversions against children were improbably common. As he had detected hysterical manifestations in himself and his siblings, he would also have had to implicate his own father, which Freud found to be less than likely.

However, he needed to account for the sexual scenes which his patients called to mind. It was in the summer of 1897, the year following his father's death, that Freud treated a man who reacted to bereavement by developing an obsessional neurosis, fearing that he would lose control of himself in the street and kill someone. This man remembered having harboured murderous feelings towards his father in childhood. He also reported dreaming of incestuous acts with his mother. Freud might have dissociated himself from such thoughts, regarding them as an idiosyncratic occurrence, but in fact he identified with the patient, detecting signs in his own dreams of sexual jealousy towards the parental couple.

This was a decisive moment, for he now came to believe that if actual sexual seduction in childhood was not ubiquitous, childhood sexual fantasy was. It is perhaps the fate of all of us, he suggested, 'to direct our first sexual impulses towards our mother and our first hatred and our first murderous wish against our father. Our dreams convince us that this is so.'[11] According to this view, hysteria was no longer inexorably linked with sexual seduction, but rather with a child's developmental difficulty in overcoming primitive jealousy. Sophocles' King Oedipus, who slew his father and married his mother, was the paradigm for every man's wish in early childhood, destined to be suppressed and unconsciously turned against the self in the form of a critical conscience.

Freud neither ceased to believe that childhood sexual abuse occurred, nor that it produced damaging psychological consequences. But he did shift the focus of his interest from the nature of the traumatic events to the way in which those events were experienced. And he came to believe that memories were not simple reproductions of the past, but open to unconscious imaginative elaboration. It has been suggested that Freud believed the 'seduction theory' to be true, and altered his opinion to placate public opinion.[12] There is little to support this view, which flies in the face of his combative character and undiminished capacity for giving offence. Indeed the new theory of infantile sexuality and Oedipal fantasy, which marked his transition from physician into psychoanalyst, has never ceased to evoke controversy.

SIX

THE INTERPRETATION OF DREAMS

*It seems to be my fate to discover only the obvious: that
children have sexual feelings, which every nursemaid
knows; and that night dreams are just as much a wish
fulfilment as day dreams*[1]

The Interpretation of Dreams was published at the
end of 1899 and postdated by Freud's publisher
to 1900. It was indeed a work bestriding the
centuries. On the one hand its psychology, couched
in the language of 'quantities of excitation',
envisaged the mind as a kind of electrostatic
machine intent on divesting itself of 'charge', and
harked back to the abandoned *Project for a Scientific
Psychology*. On the other, its virtuoso exploration of
mental life looked forward to a psychology

Freud's father Jacob, gentle Galician Jew and impecunious wool merchant (Freud Museum, London)

Freud's birthplace in a Moravian town known as Freiberg to German speakers and Příbor to Czechs. His parents occupied a single rented room at Schlossergasse 117 above the blacksmith J. Zajic (Freud Museum, London)

Martha Bernays, Freud's fiancée, in 1883 (Freud Museum, London)

The brilliant and unfortunate Ernst von Fleischl-Marxow, Freud's friend who became addicted to morphine and subsequently cocaine (Freud Museum, London)

Wilhelm Fliess, Freud's intimate confidant during the years 1890–1900 (Freud Museum, London)

Josef Breuer, physician, famous physiologist and co-author with Freud of *Studies on Hysteria*, 1893 (Freud Museum, London)

The handsome couple. Freud and Martha just after their wedding in 1886 (Freud Museum, London)

Freud in America, September 1909, to receive an honorary doctorate and deliver a course of lectures. Back row, left to right: A.A. Brill, Ernest Jones, Sandor Ferenczi; front row: Freud (with cigar), Stanley Hall (President of Clark University, Worcester, MA), C.G. Jung (Freud Museum, London)

Sigmund Freud on the balcony of his summer home, Hohe Warte, with two chows, his constant companions, 1933 (Freud Museum, London)

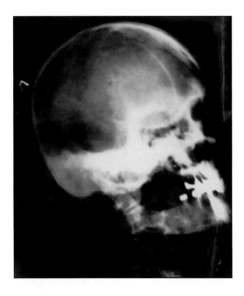

X-ray of Freud's skull showing
large gap after surgical excision of
right upper jaw and palette
(Freud Museum, London)

Freud's study in Maresfield Gardens, London, with collection of antiques brought from
Vienna and print of André Brouillet's *La Leçon clinique du Dr Charcot* above the couch
(Freud Museum, London)

Freud with grandson Stephan Gabriel, son of Ernst, in 1922
(Mary Evans Picture Library)

Freud and Anna, refugees from Nazi Austria, in Paris en route for London, 1938
(Mary Evans Picture Library)

unfettered by spurious physical explanations and, true to the deeply textured conflicts of subjective experience, the subtle mixture of memory and desire.

'Do you suppose,' Freud wondered six months after publication, 'that someday one will read on a marble tablet on this house:

> Here, on July 24, 1895,
> the secret of the dream
> revealed itself to Dr. Sigm. Freud.'[2]

It seemed extravagant at the time, for the book had been sparsely reviewed and indifferently received in medical circles. The first six hundred copies took eight years to sell out. But two years later a general readership called for a second edition and by the time of Freud's death in 1939, eight more had been produced, as well as translations into English, Russian, Spanish, French, Swedish, Japanese, Hungarian and Czech. The marble was actually inscribed in 1977, and still the book is reprinted. What was revealed to Freud on that midsummer night in 1895?

Most certainly more than he passed on to the

reader, for he makes it clear that he is reporting an edited version of 'Irma's injection', his famous specimen dream, offered as an illustration of 'disguised wish fulfilment'. As with screen memories and hysterical symptoms, Freud saw dreams as meaningful products of repressed emotion. However, where the former were originally seen to derive their force from adult sexuality, he now insisted that early sexual fantasy was projected forwards, thus imbuing current dream imagery with a 'prehistoric' significance. Given the central thesis that dreams represent the disguised fulfilment of unconscious sexual wishes (deriving from the first few years of life), it is noteworthy that the wish Freud uncovers in 'Irma's injection' is no more scurrilous than a desire to vindicate his professional reputation.

On the evening of the dream he had been hurt by the criticism of his friend 'Otto' for failing to deliver a complete cure to 'Irma'. In summary, the dream has Freud telling her that if the pain persists, it is her own fault. She continues to complain and he becomes alarmed, worrying that he may have missed something. He examines her throat and sees a big white patch and extensive grey-white scabs that resemble the turbinate bones of the nose. Dr M (Breuer) is called in, confirms the dreamer's diagnosis of infection and reassures him that dysentery will ensue and the toxin will be eliminated. Meanwhile Otto appears and another friend, 'Leopold', is percussing (tapping sharply: a medical procedure) Irma through her bodice. All present know how she got infected: it was Otto, who had administered an injection of tri-methylamin, probably using a non-sterile syringe. There is general disapproval of such thoughtless practice.

By taking each element in the dream and observing the thoughts associated with it, Freud spun a tangled web of old memories, new experiences and recent preoccupations. It was in this underlying 'latent content', that he looked for the meaning of the dream, its 'manifest content' being no more than a plausible disguise.

Among the numerous links generated, he discerned a common thread – his own guilty conscience. Thus the 'white patch' and scabs reminded him of a patient who had developed extensive necrosis of the nasal mucosa through following his example with cocaine; and hence to the whole sorry story of Fleischl, whose death, Freud felt, had been hastened by his ill-advised encouragement to experiment with the drug. Trimethylamin had been mentioned once by Fliess in a conversation concerning sexual chemistry, which led Freud to think of his own ideas about the sexual origins of hysteria. If Irma's failure to recover resulted from lack of a sexual outlet (she was a widow), then once again Freud would be vindicated. In short, by blaming others, the dream obscured Freud's sense of guilt and fulfilled his wish to be innocent of professional negligence.

Notwithstanding the unexplored sexual references, what Freud fails to say, and what seems obvious to the informed reader, is that Irma also represents Emma Eckstein, and that it is Fliess above all whom the dream exonerates from wrongdoing.

To have asserted that dreams often portray the satisfaction of longings which reality denies would have been uncontroversial. But Freud's rhetoric oscillated continually between reasonable instances of straightforward wish-fulfilment, demonstrations of dream disguises and generalisations belied by his own evidence. As with the rest of Freud's work, the reader will search in vain for consistency and coherence. Its value resides not, as he thought, in its status as a body of psychological laws, but rather in its wellspring of original ideas, stimulating challenges and erratic hypotheses.

Freud's fundamental vision highlighted the plasticity of mental functioning, our capacity to retreat from painful realities and salvage a sense of subjective well-being. This was the 'pleasure principle', which dominated unconscious mental activity (what Freud called 'primary process' thinking), and drove the dream-machine. It cocked a snook at reality, refused to be bound by logic, was untroubled by contradictions and unencumbered by limits of space and time. It produced fantasised satisfaction, but was wholly useless in meeting the practical needs of life, unless translated into the 'reality principle' by ordinary conscious ('secondary process') thinking.

Dreams, therefore, were regressive states tending towards the primary process, the 'royal road'[3] to the unconscious mind; but at the same time they did take account of standards and values, hence the compromise and the disguise. They took their signposts from the random occurrences of daily life and made them point in two directions at once, to an incoherent but personally unobjectionable story − the manifest dream, and to an underlying narrative imbued with primitive passions and unacceptable desires.

Although the hidden author of the dream must have 'known' the truth, he employed clever devices ('dream-work') in order to obscure it from his alter ego. 'Condensation' enabled one dream image to make reference to a plurality of underlying ideas, 'displacement' allowed the emotion appropriate to one idea to be shifted on to a seemingly irrelevant one, and symbolic substitutions provided for a further degree of ambiguity. In addition, any element was held to be capable of representing its opposite, since the unconscious primary process had no means of expressing negation. Finally, the contents were subject to 'secondary revision': given a gloss of coherence in order to make the story plausible. All dreams bore 'the mark of the beast',[4] Freud averred; none were guileless.

Naturally such a gauntlet was taken up by patients, readers and critics alike, who proceeded to furnish Freud with counter-examples − dreams of painful and frightening experiences which could not possibly have been desired. And, one by one, Freud supplied the answers. The wish is latent, not manifest; a woman who dreams that she wants to give a supper but cannot find the food is satisfying her wish to refrain from inviting a friend of whom her husband is fond and she is jealous; a woman who dreams that her fifteen-year-old daughter is lying dead in a box is satisfying her earlier wish for an abortion when pregnant; the experience of anxiety is the distorted satisfaction of a sexual desire, and so on. It is typical of Freud to have claimed enthusiastically that the accuracy of this last statement 'has been demonstrated with ever increasing certainty',[5] and equally characteristic that he himself was subsequently to reject the theory as untenable. When confronted by dreams whose content would not yield to any interpretive manoeuvre, Freud played his trump card – the latent wish of the dreamer was to prove him wrong!

Freud's controversial ideas concerning the role of infantile sexuality in later life may have delayed his advancement in the academic world, but the rise of political anti-Semitism was probably a stronger factor. In 1897 the demagogue Karl Lueger had become Mayor of Vienna, basing his popularity on an appeal to Jew-hatred. The culture of equal opportunity rapidly declined, making preferment even more difficult for the unbaptised. In the same year Freud's nomination for the title of Professor Extraordinarius (endorsed by the medical faculty of the University of Vienna), remained inexplicably unratified by the Ministry of Education.

Naively hoping for a better outcome in succeeding years, Freud waited patiently for the title he deserved, but nothing happened. Then in 1902, following a visit to Rome, he decided to become proactive. Rome held a special significance for Freud; he dreamt of it repeatedly. He had always longed to visit the city yet found himself prevented from doing so by neurotic inhibitions. On one occasion, while planning a detour, he was suddenly reminded of his youthful identification with Hannibal, who had been fated not to enter Rome. He realised that, for him, Rome was the locus of an emotional conflict. It symbolised ancient culture and all that he admired in Enlightenment European civilisation, but also the Catholic Church, and by extension the anti-Semitic Austrian Establishment, whose prejudice stood in the way of his ambitions. It is no coincidence that, having overcome his travel phobia, he should have felt free to take steps to secure his professorship.

Freud consulted his old teacher Sigmund von Exner, who reluctantly conceded that personal influences with His Excellency were acting against Freud and advised him to employ 'counter-influence'. Freud then enlisted the support of an influential former patient, Elise Gomperz, wife of the eminent classicist Theodor Gomperz, who spoke to the minister on his behalf. The minister, however, feigned ignorance of the whole affair and it looked as though nothing would come of it. In the meantime another of Freud's patients, Baroness Marie Ferstel, whose husband had been appointed consul-general in Berlin, got to hear of the matter. She gained the ear of the minister, invited him to dinner and donated a painting to an art gallery he was planning to set up. On 22 February 1902, Freud, at the age of forty-five, had a wife and six children, had invented psychoanalysis, succeeded in visiting Rome, and was duly conferred with the title Professor Extraordinarius by Emperor Franz Josef.

Public acclaim had at last arrived, and congratulations and flowers poured in. It was as if 'the role of sexuality has suddenly been officially recognised by His Majesty, the significance of the dream certified by the Council of Ministers, and the necessity of a psychoanalytic therapy of hysteria carried by a two-thirds majority in Parliament,'[6] he wryly commented.

SEVEN

THE PSYCHOANALYTIC MOVEMENT

There are still so few of us that disagreements, based perhaps on personal 'complexes', ought to be excluded among us[1]

Freud's professorial status owed more to his early research in neuroanatomy than it did to any general acceptance of his psychoanalytical innovations. Despite the newly acquired rank, his focus of intellectual activity remained firmly outside Vienna University. Nevertheless, through clinical practice, writing and lectures, psychoanalytical ideas were gradually becoming known to a small group of physicians. These avante-garde young doctors were fascinated by the 'free speech' psychoanalysis championed, and the social implications of its liberation philosophy, though they did not always interpret this in the same way as Freud, who was far from being a sexual libertine.

Wilhelm Stekel, poet, musician and medical practitioner, had been briefly and successfully treated by Freud for a psycho-sexual problem, most likely impotence. It was his suggestion which prompted Freud, in autumn 1902, to invite colleagues to a regular meeting on Wednesday evenings at his home. Max Kahane (who, like Freud, had translated Charcot into German), Rudolf Reitler and Alfred Adler, a socialist physician active in community work, were the other founding members of the 'Wednesday Psychological Society'. Together they formed a corporate replacement for Fliess in Freud's life.

It was an informal gathering of like-minded thinkers (or so it at first seemed), dedicated to the open exchange of new ideas in the field. Each week someone would present a paper and, after a short break for black coffee and cakes, a discussion would be held. Cigarettes and cigars would be smoked and finally Freud, acting as chairman, would sum up the evening's work. New recruits were introduced by existing members and, in the early days, invariably accepted with unanimous consent. The atmosphere was congenial, the conversation compelling.

By 1906 the membership had risen to seventeen and included the doctors Isidor Sadger and his nephew Fritz Wittels, Paul Federn and Eduard Hitschmann, as well as non-medical people such as Max Graf, the musicologist, Hugo Heller, the publisher, and most extraordinarily Otto Rank, a self-taught 21-year-old machinist, whom Adler (his GP) introduced, and Freud took under his wing. Rank was persuaded to pursue his education as a mature student at the gymnasium and university, but he had already written a small book on the cultural application of psychoanalysis and was working on another concerning the incest motive in literature. In 1905 he was given the paid post of secretary to the society, and made responsible for recording attendance, keeping financial accounts and taking comprehensive notes on each meeting.

During this period, Freud produced several important books which extended the application of psychoanalytical principles, begun in the *Interpretation of Dreams*, to other intriguing aspects of normal life – slips of the tongue and pen, loss of memory for particular words or events, jokes, inexplicable mistakes and apparently unintentional gestures. All were ingeniously reframed in terms of unconscious intent.[2]

In 1905 Freud published *Three Essays on the Theory of Sexuality*,[3] which spelled out his views on the nature of unconscious life, as a kind of hidden park for partially extinct sexual themes. Interweaving Fliessian notions of bisexuality with the prevailing view that infantile development from conception onwards was a small-scale recapitulation of the evolutionary process, Freud put forward a diphasic view of sexual growth. We were all essentially primitive 'polymorphously perverse' animals in infancy, passing through oral, anal and genital phases, and then a latent period of suppressed sexual expression lasting until the onset of puberty. However much this theory linked the evolution of adult human sexuality to a movement *away* from primitive 'animality', it was threatening enough to perpetuate the furore surrounding Freud, and cement the experience within the group of being a heroic minority dedicated to revealing unpalatable truths.

In the course of the next couple of years, a number of foreign visitors, destined to become major figures in the history of psychoanalysis, made contact with the society. Max Eitingon, a Russian Jew studying medicine in Zurich, was first to arrive in early 1907, followed by his superiors from the Burghölzli Mental Hospital, Ludwig Binswanger and Carl Gustav Jung, and at the end of the year, Karl Abraham.

Freud was delighted with his new 'Swiss' adherents, whose interest ensured the dissemination of psychoanalysis beyond Vienna. In particular he took to Jung, who adopted a filial posture towards him and had the added advantage of being Gentile. He seemed the ideal person to protect psychoanalysis from the hostile charge of being a 'Jewish science' and carry it into the future with more universal appeal.

However, the arrival of the newcomers did nothing to dampen the in-fighting with which the Wednesday Society was now beset. Nor were the new members impressed by the quality of Freud's Viennese associates. Conveying his impression of the physicians to Eitingon, Abraham described Sadger as a Talmud-disciple, Stekel superficial, Adler one-sided, Wittels too much the phrasemonger, and the others insignificant. Freud, too, was becoming impatient with the 'gang'. Stekel, whose ideas concerning dream symbolism he had enthusiastically embraced, was now an embarrassment. He seemed to invent case histories to suit himself, take a prurient interest in those of others, and be altogether too big for his boots. Affecting a self-deprecating attitude, he was fond of expressing his contribution by saying that a dwarf on the shoulder of a giant could see further than the giant himself. When told of this, Freud's withering rejoinder was 'That may be true, but a louse on the head of an astronomer does not.'[4]

If Stekel's faults proved insufferable, Jung's, though equally damning to the reputation of the psychoanalytic movement, were the subject of benign forbearance. He had been conducting a passionate affair with one of his patients, a young medical student named Sabina Spielrein. When his wife informed Spielrein's mother, who protested to Jung, he abruptly terminated the relationship. Spielrein responded with a violent knife attack on Jung, and wrote to Freud seeking a consultation and giving details of the whole episode. Not wishing to think ill of his friend, Freud was at first disinclined to believe her story. Jung tried to cover up, outrageously justifying his conduct to Spielrein's mother on the grounds that he received no fee for her daughter's treatment, and blaming her for seducing him. When the truth came out, Jung had to admit his ignoble conduct, conceding to Freud it was 'a piece of knavery which I very reluctantly confess to you as my father'.[5]

In February 1908, having been recruited by Jung, the open-hearted Hungarian GP, Sándor Ferenczi (formerly Fränkel), joined the circle which was shortly to become the Vienna Psychoanalytic Society. And in May, Ernest Jones, a young Welsh neurologist, and Dr Abraham A. Brill from the United States, were guests of the newly constituted body. Of the early members, Eitingon and Abraham went on to establish psychoanalysis in Berlin, Ferenczi founded the Budapest Psychoanalytic Society, and Jones and Brill brought psychoanalysis to the English-speaking world.

The schismatics, Adler, Stekel and Jung, were another matter, but when the first International Psychoanalytic Congress was held in Salzburg later that year, they were all still on board.

Freud felt ostracised by the medical and academic establishment. Notwithstanding his typical

Eurocentric anti-Americanism, it came as a welcome surprise when G. Stanley Hall, President of Clark University, Massachusetts, invited him to accept the degree of Doctor of Laws, *honoris causa*. Together with Jung and Ferenczi, he was to help celebrate the twenty-fifth anniversary of the university's foundation, by delivering a course of lectures. On 21 August 1909, the three colleagues set sail from Bremen on the *George Washington*. The previous day, however, an apparently trivial but portentous event had occurred, indicating that all was not well in Freud's relationship with his 'crown prince'.

It was during lunch while waiting to embark that Jung, apparently still embarrassed by Freud's unsolicited knowledge of the Spielrein affair, started to behave in a hostile manner. Freud became irritated when he kept talking about the mummified corpses of 'peat-bog men', recently found in north Germany. The irritation grew into agitation, and finally Freud fainted. According to Jung, Freud later accused him of harbouring a death-wish against him, signified by the subject of the conversation.

Nonetheless, on returning from a successful tour of America, it was Jung whom Freud installed as

President of the International Psycho-Analytic Association in 1910, writing to Ferenczi later that year, 'I am more convinced than ever that he is the man of the future'.[6] As a sop to the Viennese, he retired from the presidency of the Vienna Society, appointing Adler in his place, and founded a new monthly periodical, *Zentralblatt für Psychoanalyse* (*Central Journal for Psychoanalysis*), to be jointly edited by Adler and Stekel; Jung was already the editor of the *Jahrbuch* (yearbook). It was a doomed manoeuvre, which did nothing to diminish the smouldering discontent of all concerned.

From Freud's point of view, Adler was moving steadily away from the central tenet of psychoanalytic theory – the unconscious repression of libido as a cause for neurosis. Instead he laid emphasis on the individual's striving to overcome feelings of inferiority. Freud considered the former to have been established as fact, the latter uncorroborated speculation. But he was not above turning Adler's idea against its author, who had announced in public, 'Do you think it gives me such great pleasure to stand in your shadow my whole life long?'[7]

The disputes came to a head in discussions held

during February 1911, and despite the best efforts of other members to broker a compromise, Adler's position as president became untenable, and he resigned at the end of the month. In May, Freud demanded his resignation as co-editor of the *Zentralblatt*, thus precipitating his departure to found the reproachfully named 'Society for Free Psychoanalysis', later to become the 'Society for Individual Psychology'.

Stekel had resigned his position as vice-president when Adler stepped down, but he continued with his editorial duties into the following year, in an atmosphere of persisting acrimony. Freud interfered in the running of the journal, insisting that the lawyer, Viktor Tausk, be appointed as book-review editor. When Stekel resisted this incursion into his editorial autonomy, Freud wrote to the publisher in an attempt to get him removed, and finally persuaded everyone else associated with the journal to resign, leaving Stekel in charge of an empty shell. The *Internationale Zeitschrift* was then founded to replace the *Zentralblatt*. To Freud's evident relief, Stekel resigned from the Vienna Society on 6 November 1912.

Unbeknown to Stekel (and Jung), and at Ernest

Jones's suggestion, a secret committee ha
formed earlier that year, to protect psychoa
from deviationist trends. Jones had proposed t
small group of 'Old Guard' colleagues would give
Freud moral support if future conflict threatened,
and help in supplying material to substantiate basic
theories. Freud's predilection for clandestine
arrangements made the idea a certain winner.
Accordingly, Jones, Ferenczi, Abraham, Rank,
Hanns Sachs, and later Eitingon, decided to form an
unofficial cabal.

In the meantime, Freud's inflated estimation of
Jung had ineluctably burst. Not only was he remiss in
carrying out the administrative duties of his office, but
his doctrinal deviations were increasingly apparent,
and ultimately aired publicly in his Fordham Lectures,
given in NewYork in September 1912.

Jung had, in fact, turned the 'Oedipus Complex'
upside down. Infantile sexuality, the touchstone of
psychoanalysis, had been severed from its biological
roots, becoming for him an ethereal manifestation
of primordial myth. It was not infantile sexual
fantasy that determined adult neurosis, but rather
current difficulties in adult life that reactivated
prehistoric conflicts.

For his part, Jung accused Freud of being intolerant to dissent and playing the critical father. He admitted harbouring mixed feelings, but the more hostility Freud read into his behaviour, the angrier he became. Eventually, following a bitter exchange of letters, Freud wrote to Jung on 3 January 1913, proposing 'that we abandon our personal relations entirely'. Three days later, 'The rest is silence,' Jung replied.[8]

WAR AND DEATH

*It might be said that we owe the fairest flowerings of our
love to the reaction against the hostile impulse which we
sense within us*[1]

In contrast to his emotional ups and downs with
his colleagues, Freud's life at home followed an
unruffled routine which, like the wider European
order, was about to be shattered by the First World
War.

Each day he would rise at seven, and after a cold
shower and visit by the barber to trim his beard, he
would take a quick breakfast and scan the
newspaper. At eight he saw his first patient, with
whom he spent fifty-five minutes. Thereafter
patients came on the hour till one o'clock, when the
family had their main meal. After lunch, he would
go for a walk, deliver manuscripts to his publisher
and buy cigars and other necessities. At three, he
would put on his frock coat and see new patients.

He conducted more analytic sessions between four and nine, when he had a break for supper. Afterwards he would go for a stroll with Martha, Minna or one of the children, often dropping into a café. He stayed up till the early hours of the morning, writing papers and dealing with correspondence.

The weeks were also mapped out. Apart from the Wednesday meetings of the Psychoanalytic Society, on alternate Tuesday evenings he attended the B'nai B'rith, the Jewish Fellowship he had joined in 1897. Saturday nights were devoted to playing taroc – a card game derived from the Jewish mystical cabbalistic tradition – with friends, and on Sunday mornings he visited his mother with the children; in the afternoon he often received visitors, and in the evening his mother returned to dine at his house.

Summer holidays were a delight for the extended Freud family, spent at the seaside or more often in the mountains. Freud's son Martin recalls his earliest experience of a visit to the Adriatic coast, a few months before his youngest sister, Anna, was born. His father and Uncle Alexander were enjoying their swim so much that they refused to come ashore for lunch; whereupon a waiter was despatched to wade out, balancing a tray with refreshments, cigars and matches. Such carefree vacations continued into the first decade of the new century, but the idyll was about to end.

When war broke out in July 1914, Freud's children were all grown up. Mathilde had been married for six years to Robert Hollitscher, a business man; and Sophie had married Max Halberstadt, a Hamburg photographer, the previous year. They already had a four-month-old baby boy, Freud's first grandchild.

Martin, then a young lawyer, volunteered to serve in the artillery and was posted to the Russian front. Oliver, then training as an engineer, and Ernst, as an architect, were both later to be involved in active service. Anna, eighteen years old and intending to become a schoolteacher, was stranded on holiday in Freud's beloved England, discomfitingly now on 'the wrong side'. She made her way back to Vienna accompanied by the Austrian ambassador.

Like most people across Europe, Freud greeted the war with a surge of patriotic fervour, a sense of solidarity with Germany and the Central Powers, which he had scarcely thought possible. Ferenczi too, in the Hungarian Hussars, wrote cheeringly that he had conducted the first 'hippic psychoanalysis'[2] while riding on horseback with his commandant. But it did not take long before the realities began to strike home. With three sons, two sons-in-law and a nephew at risk, his practice decimated and his young psychoanalytic colleagues drafted into military service, Freud's thoughts turned to darker considerations. This was the period when he produced *Mourning and Melancholia, Thoughts for the Times on War and Death*, and a series of brilliant essays summarising his work on the unconscious mind, which he now called 'metapsychology'.

In *Mourning and Melancholia*, he took a first step in understanding the way mixed feelings towards a loved person are dealt with. Having observed that both mourning and depressive states were related to loss (or anticipated loss), and often both conditions were accompanied by self-reproach, he proposed that it was the lost person to whom the reproachful feelings were truly directed. His or her identity had been preserved by incorporating it into the grieving person's self. For this reason, mourners frequently found themselves acquiring the habits and behaviours previously belonging to the dead. The unconscious ambivalence in the relationship during life now became an internal affair, pathologically prolonged in cases of melancholia. It was a psychological mechanism – 'identification with a lost object' – which was to form a crucial part of Freud's later thinking.

In wartime it is tempting to perceive the enemy as uniformly bad and one's own side as good, but Freud's ruthless self-scrutiny could not allow such tendentious habits of mind. If psychoanalysis was characterised by anything, it was the willingness to acknowledge home truths – hatred, aggression and overweening egotism, even against one's own kin. What fascinated Freud, however, was the way that, given favourable conditions, such primitive urges were somehow transformed and employed in the service of love.

During the night of 8 July 1915, Freud dreamt that he had received good news concerning Martin. The officer's mess 'had sent a sum of money (5,000 Kronen?) . . . something about distinction . . . distribution . . .',[3] but in the dream his wife reacted with alarm and refused to listen. It seemed clear, on waking, that the 'good' news was a thin disguise covering up the dream's underlying message – that Martin had been killed. No doubt such an anxiety was natural enough (in fact Martin was wounded several days later), yet Freud was not content to see the dream as an unalloyed expression of parental concern. He noted that, later in the dream, Martin climbed on to a basket, and this reminded him of an occasion when he had himself, as a small boy, climbed on a stool to reach something and hurt himself falling off. The memory was accompanied by the thought, 'that serves you right', which Freud did not shrink from interpreting as 'a hostile impulse aimed at the gallant soldier'.[4]

Here we can see his unsparing self-analysis at work. Not only was he willing to see the dream as a token of hostile impulses against his beloved son, but he went on: 'Deeper analysis at last enabled me to discover what the concealed impulse was which might have found satisfaction in the dreaded accident to my son: it was the envy which is felt for the young by those who have grown old, but which they believe they have completely stifled.'[5] What war brought home to Freud was the universal ease with which the restraints of civilisation are cast off, and the murderous impulses set free.

It was difficult to keep the psychoanalytic movement alive during the war. International congresses fell into abeyance, but the Vienna Society managed to meet every three weeks, and Freud preserved the *Zeitschrift* by doing most of the work himself. There were shortages of food and fuel, which meant his study could not be heated in winter and his fingers became too cold to write.

Freud was now in his sixties, suffering from rheumatism and prostate trouble, which caused urinary difficulties. The earnings from his practice were unreliable. At the beginning of 1917 he had no patients and prices were rising fast. The war looked lost and in the summer his nephew was killed on the Italian front. Rank was suffering a severe depression and Ferenczi was found to have tuberculosis and thyroid disease. Writing to Karl Abraham, Freud confessed, 'I have been working very hard, feel worn out and am beginning to find the world repellently loathsome. The superstition that my life is due to finish in February 1918 often seems to me quite a friendly idea.'[6]

Counter to superstition, 1918 actually proved a better year. With the help of financial support from a wealthy Hungarian patient, Dr Phil Anton von

Freund, Freud was able to set up an independent publishing house, the *Verlag*; and in September Abraham organised a successful International Psychoanalytic Congress at Budapest. It was the first to have taken place since the outbreak of war, and was attended by high-ranking medical officers from Austria, Germany and Hungary, who had grown interested in the application of psychoanalytical ideas to the treatment of war neuroses. Ferenczi was elected president and it was also decided that undergoing a personal analysis should be a requirement for future psychoanalytical training – an idea, not inappropriately, first mooted by Jung many years before. This was a landmark decision, for till then an interest and acquaintance with Freud's work, supplemented in some cases by the briefest exposure to personal analysis, had sufficed.

The new rule meant that Anna, the only one of Freud's children drawn to psychoanalysis as a career, would need to undergo an analytic experience before being admitted to the International Psychoanalytic Association. For the delicate role of training analyst, Freud selected himself.

Anna's analysis with her father was conducted between 1918 and 1921. These were years of physical deprivation and extreme hardship. Living in unheated rooms, off a diet which consisted almost entirely of thin vegetable soup, Freud continued to work by his couch, clad in overcoat and gloves. At one point, he wrote an article for a Hungarian periodical, for which he requested payment in potatoes.

Unbeknown to his anxious parents, Martin had been taken prisoner by the Italians at the end of the war, but it was not until March 1919 that they first heard news of him from a Red Cross postcard. All Freud's sons had survived, but in a cruel twist, within six months of Martin's return, his sister Sophie, pregnant with her third child, unexpectedly succumbed to the postwar flu epidemic.

Anna went to Hamburg to be with her grieving brother-in-law and two young nephews, Ernstl and Heinele. It was while staying with them, listening with an analytic ear to the six-year-old Ernstl's stories, that she took her first steps in child analysis. She was able to link his fear of the dark to the associated fear of handling his penis, which his mother had warned him against. Masturbation guilt and its psychological consequences was a recurring theme in her later work.

In May 1922, after reading a paper on sado-masochistic fantasies, probably derived from her own experience, Anna was admitted into the Vienna Psychoanalytic Society. Together with the Hungarian-born Melanie Klein (also the daughter of a physician), who had been in analysis with both Ferenczi and Abraham, she was to pioneer the application of psychoanalysis to children, carrying its torch into the second half of the twentieth century.

Anna's own sexuality was a source of concern to her father. Writing to his dear friend and female colleague, Lou Andreas-Salomé in May 1924, shortly after resuming Anna's analysis, he confided, 'The child gives me enough worries: how she will bear the lonely life [after Freud's death], and whether I can drive her libido from the hiding place into which it has crawled.'[7] Anna was twenty-nine years old, and Freud fervently hoped that analysis would liberate her from celibacy (and her 'father complex'), but did not seem to realise that he was the last person to be able to undertake such a task. His little 'Black Devil', who had become his 'dear only daughter' when her sisters left home, grew ever fonder of her father – becoming his closest colleague, devoted amanuensis and indispensable sick nurse, guarding her roles with increasing jealousy as time went by.

NINE

EGO AND ID

Dear Incorrigible Optimist,
Tampon renewed today. Out of bed. What is left of me put
into clothes. Thanks for all the news, letters, greetings, and
newspaper cuttings. As soon as I can sleep without an
injection I shall go home[1]

When Freud tried to give up smoking, he was unable to work. As early as 1895 he wrote to Fliess explaining how he relapsed after fourteen months' abstinence, during which he constantly missed it: 'I must treat this psychic fellow well or he won't work for me. I demand a great deal of him. The torment, most of the time, is superhuman.'[2] Now, nearly thirty years later, the somatic fellow was to pay the price.

At the beginning of 1923, not long after the birth of his fifth grandson, Lucien (destined to become a great painter), Freud noticed a white growth on the right side of his jaw and palate, which he took to be

cancerous. Despite reassurances from Marcus
Hajek, the first surgeon he consulted, when the
growth was excised and examined Freud's
suspicions proved to be correct. Hajek continued to
equivocate about the diagnosis, while at the same
time arranging further treatment with radiotherapy,
then in its infancy. The dosage must have been
erratic and associated damage to healthy tissue
painful. By September it was evident that more
major surgery would be necessary, since the cancer
was clearly invasive.

On 4 and 11 October Professor Hans Pichler, a
distinguished oral surgeon, performed a two-stage
operation under local anaesthetic, in which the
whole of the right side of Freud's upper jaw and
palate were removed. A huge prosthesis, nick-
named 'the monster', was required to replace the
bone and shut off the mouth from the gaping nasal
cavity, so that Freud could eat and speak.

During the sixteen years that followed the
diagnosis of his cancer, Freud underwent thirty-
three operations, in an attempt to control its
spread. As a result he became deaf in his right ear,
and suffered from recurrent infections and enduring
pain. Eating was difficult and his speech became

defective, varying according to the fit of the prosthesis. Throughout this prolonged ordeal Anna nursed him, aided by her mother and aunt, and he continued to work.

But in June 1923 there was a misery that rent his spirits even more than the discovery of his own cancer. It was the death from miliary tuberculosis of his little grandson Heinele, the orphaned child of Sophie. Freud loved the boy dearly, and his death stirred a deep well of grief — Freud wept for his daughter, his grandson, himself, and for all humanity.

Three years earlier, in *Beyond the Pleasure Principle*, he had mooted the idea of a death instinct, an inherent drive towards disintegration and destruction, balanced against the libidinal, life-affirming forces. It was a speculation that met with little enthusiasm among colleagues, but his doleful concurrence with the pessimistic philosophy of Friedrich Schopenhauer — that *'the aim of all life is death'*[3] — must now have seemed brutally confirmed.

Freud's long years of practice had familiarised him with self-destructive behaviour, often unconsciously repeated in successive relationships. His recognition of punishment-seeking behaviour, and unconscious *resistance* to free association and therapeutic progress, indicated that the domain of the unconscious mind was no pleasure dome.

If his earlier theorising had been characterised by the vicissitudes of pleasure-seeking, Freud's mature map of the mind was equally concerned with the origin of ascetic self-punishing forces. His last major synthesis, *The Ego and the Id*, appeared in the same year as his 'tissue rebellion',[4] and reconceptualised mental conflict into a tripartite struggle.

After all the fuss surrounding his concept of 'the unconscious', Freud in his later years swept it aside as a mere 'symptom', or state that any of the mind's components might happen to be in. The fundamental conflict was not conscious versus unconscious, but instinctual drives (the *id*) versus internal interdictions (the *superego*) and the limitations to gratification imposed by external reality. It was the unenviable task of the *ego* to reconcile the conflicting forces, judge their competing claims and execute appropriate behaviour. In doing so it bore the same power relationship to the id as did a rider to a horse, engaging in all sorts of subtle strategies in order to divert the id's energy to its own purposes.

The struggle to become a person was a struggle to replace the automatic responses programmed by our biological development with individual responses determined by our selves – 'Where id was, there ego shall be', became the motto of the psychoanalytic endeavour.[5] Freud interwove this new 'structural' model of the mind with his existing theories concerning the phasic development of libido in an ingenious way. Man's superego, or conscience, was neither God-given nor inculcated by strict schooling; it was a natural product of frustrated infantile love and distorted infantile fantasy.

A small boy tended to identify with his father, but suffered *castration anxiety*, exacerbated by the first sight of the female genitals. Perceiving his father as a jealous rival, he was thrown into conflict, ultimately withdrawing his claims on the mother and replacing her with an imaginary entity or 'internal parent', rather in the same way as a mourner identified with a lost love. It was a kind of psychological 'protection racket', where anxiety over confrontation with the father was diminished, at the price of long-term submission to the foibles of a couple of fantasised moralists which Freud called the superego. In this way the Oedipus complex was resolved.

The new story was not completely coherent. As well as being 'heir to the Oedipus Complex', the superego was the product of 'organic repression', deriving from supposed guilty memories of a primeval patricide, passed through the generations by Lamarckian inheritance. And since the unconscious was bisexual, the male pattern of internalisation was mirrored by a parallel but different process in its female part.

But Freud's phallocentric account of normal female development was by his own admission unsatisfactory, and led to the prejudicial claim that women's ethical sense was inferior to that of men. Since the formation of the superego was supposedly driven by castration anxiety, little girls (who perceived themselves as castrated boys) had nothing to lose. They grew up envying their brothers' genitals, but at the same time were not driven, through fear, to relinquish their attachment to the parent of the opposite sex (*pace* Anna), and consequently had less need to internalise a conscience!

Nobody believes this to be an adequate account of female development, nor does it square with Freud's own relationships with women and respect for female colleagues in the psychoanalytic movement (at a time when women were generally unwelcome in political and professional life).

Lou Andreas-Salomé, wife of the orientalist Friedrich Carl Andreas and lover of brilliant men (among whom were numbered the philosopher Friedrich Nietzsche and the poet Rainer Maria Rilke), was a regular guest of the Vienna Psychoanalytic Society from 1912. There is no suggestion that her relationship with Freud was romantic, but she became a friend and colleague, as did his former patients Emma Eckstein, Sabina Spielrein (after leaving Jung), and Princess Marie Bonaparte.

These early pioneers were intellectual women of a special ilk, who had liberated themselves from bourgeois social constraints and saw psychoanalysis as an instrument of personal freedom. But, over the years, Freud's ill-chosen comments in *Some Psychical Consequences of the Anatomical Distinction between the Sexes* have given offence to thousands of women and, for many unforgiving feminists, turned him into a patriarchal bogey-man.

In contrast to Freud's alleged intransigence, when disharmony began to appear in his committee of stalwarts, he bent over backwards to accommodate the conflict. It was always difficult to decide whether innovations in the theory and technique of psychoanalysis were to be considered legitimate extensions or heretical deviations. In 1923, while he was struggling with his cancer, Rank and Ferenczi published *The Development of Psychoanalysis*, a book in which they emphasised the importance of analysing a patient's present actions (as well as past memories). Freud embraced the work as a major contribution, whereas Jones and Abraham remained circumspect.

Later the same year, Rank published *The Trauma of Birth*, a book to match Freud's grandest speculations with one of his own – the aim of life was to 'undo the trauma of birth',[6] and neurosis supervened when this proved impossible. The job of analysis was to sort out mother–infant conflicts arising from this, and allow the patient to be born again. No matter that this seemed to undermine the essential role of the Oedipus complex in psychoanalytic thinking, Freud urged open-minded tolerance on his doubting disciples.

The centre could not hold. In 1925 Abraham, Rank's bitterest critic, died of cancer of the lung, at the untimely age of forty-eight, shortly after he had crossed swords with Freud over his role in authorising G.W. Pabst's popular psychoanalytic film, *Secrets of the Soul*. Rank vacillated in his commitment, claiming to have superseded Freudian ideas but then making peace; his deviation was attributed to manic depression. Nonetheless, in 1926 he broke definitively with the psychoanalytic movement.

As for Ferenczi, Freud became ever more concerned over his development of an 'active', short-term technique, designed to replace a bad mothering experience with a good one. He had reason to be doubtful. In 1911 Ferenczi had taken his lover Gizella Altschul's 24-year-old daughter, Elma, into analysis. He soon became involved in an emotional quagmire, from which Freud was unable to extricate him. Becoming Gizella's husband scarcely resolved their problems. By 1927 she was suggesting divorce, so that Ferenczi could marry her daughter.

Little wonder that when Clara Thompson, one of Ferenczi's patients, broadcast the news that 'I am allowed to kiss Papa Ferenczi as often as I like',[7] Freud reacted with cautionary concern. Stung by his admonitions, Ferenczi became increasingly withdrawn. In 1932, Freud tried to persuade Ferenczi out of his 'isolation' by getting him to take on the presidency of the International Psychoanalytic Association, but he stepped down at the last moment and Jones took the post. Ferenczi was in fact ill with undiagnosed pernicious anaemia, from which he was to die the following May.

Just as his inner circle diminished and his own physical condition deteriorated, Freud began to acquire honours. He had been unsuccessfully nominated for the Nobel Prize several times since 1917, and to be granted the 'Freedom of the City' of Vienna in 1924 was scarcely a consolation. Then at the age of seventy-four he was awarded the coveted Goethe Prize by the lord mayor of Frankfurt, which Anna accepted on his behalf. 'A nation that produced Goethe,' he had remarked earlier that year to the American ambassador, W.C. Bullitt, 'could not possibly go to the bad.'

On 12 September 1930, Freud's mother died at the age of ninety-five. It was a merciful release, for she had been suffering severely from gangrene of the leg. Freud felt no grief, no pain, just a strange sense of liberation: 'I was not allowed to die as long as she was alive, and now I may.'[8] But his time had not yet come.

In his eightieth year, Harvard University wanted to celebrate its tercentenary by conferring an honorary doctorate on Freud, but was advised that he would be unable to accept due to advanced age and poor health. Not wishing the glory to pass to another faculty, the psychology committee chose Jung instead. 'O! that estates, degrees, and offices,\ Were not deriv'd corruptly, and that clear honour\ Were purchased by the merit of the wearer',[9] Freud may have thought.

FREUD'S LEGACY

*One feels inclined to doubt sometimes whether the dragons
of primeval days are really extinct*[1]

If Freud had been concerned to achieve medical
recognition for psychoanalysis and establish it as a
respectable profession, he was equally intent on
preserving it as an independent discipline, with its
own educational requirements, training procedures
and quality control. From early days he had
encouraged non-medical members of the Vienna
Society, one of whom was Theodor Reik, a student
of French literature.

Reik first made contact with Freud in 1911,
sending his thesis on Flaubert's *The Temptation of
Saint Anthony*, which had been criticised by teachers
for its psychoanalytic orientation. When the two
men met, Reik discovered that Freud 'knew
Flaubert's book much better than I',[2] and they
discussed it at length. Freud was impressed with

Reik's character and literary intelligence, seeing him as a potential asset to psychoanalysis. Dissuading him from a career in medicine, Freud not only introduced him to the Vienna Psychoanalytic Society, but also provided financial support to the impoverished young man.

By the mid-1920s Reik was a practising analyst, but he was still dependent on receiving referrals from Freud, whose reputation attracted a steady stream of English and American patients (capable of paying in hard currency) to the economically ravaged city.

In 1925 an American physician named Newton Murphy came to Vienna seeking analysis with Freud. Having no vacancies, Freud referred him on to his junior colleague, with unfortunate results. Within a few weeks, Murphy was so dissatisfied that he commenced court proceedings against Reik.

Since Austrian law prohibited 'the unauthorized pursuit of medical practice', Reik's case raised fundamental questions concerning the nature of psychoanalysis and its clinical standing, which were to split the movement (and recur in other countries) for years to come. Freud's view was unequivocal – a medical degree was not necessary to the practice of psychoanalysis (and could even be a handicap), but medical knowledge was required in selecting suitable cases for treatment, and ensuring that their symptoms did not betoken an organic illness. Lay analysts should therefore only take patients who had first been assessed by the medically qualified.

Reik's predicament galvanised Freud into action. In one month he wrote a persuasive tract, *The Question of Lay Analysis*, elegantly stating his argument in the form of a Platonic dialogue – perhaps the most accessible account of psychoanalysis he had produced. His intervention helped to establish that Reik was not a quack, and in May 1927 Murphy's evidence was finally thrown out of court. 'As long as I live,' Freud had passionately declared, 'I shall balk at having psychoanalysis swallowed by medicine.'[3] But there were more sinister dangers shortly to unfold.

On 30 January 1933, Hitler became Chancellor of Germany, and within a few months had subverted all the democratic institutions of state to his own despotic purposes. Freedom ceased to exist, and Jews were prevented from serving on public bodies and scientific councils. Two of Freud's sons, Oliver and Ernst, then living in the Weimar Republic, migrated to France and England respectively. Most of the German psychoanalysts fled the country, including Max Eitingon, who emigrated to Jerusalem, where he founded a psychoanalytical society.

On 10 May there were huge bonfires in the squares of cities and university towns, where literature proscribed by the Nazi regime was publicly burned. Students and professors alike joined in the mass repudiation of liberal culture. Work by Social Democrat politicians, poets, novelists and scientists, most particularly Jews such as Heinrich Heine, Karl Marx, Franz Kafka, Albert Einstein and Freud, was consigned to the flames. It was an omen whose evil indications were beyond imagination.

When the Nazis insisted that the policies of the German-based International Society for Psychotherapy, and the *Zentralblatt für Psychotherapie*, conform to their doctrines, its president, Dr Ernst Kretschmer, resigned, to be replaced by Jung. In 1936, he was joined by Professor H.M. Goering, cousin of the Reichsmarshal, as co-editor of the journal. At the same time, the central depot of the psychoanalytic publishing house in Leipzig was seized by the Gestapo. Ernest Jones's protest that it belonged to an international body, sent from England by cable to the chief of police in Leipzig, was of no avail. As a result the *Verlag* had to relocate in Vienna, where it continued to function on a reduced scale for the following two years.

Jung justified his continued collaboration with the Nazis in these difficult times, on grounds of expediency. He did his best to save individual Jews. But his personal hostility to Freud, general antipathy to free-thinking 'Jewish' rationalism, wavering admiration for Hitler's thaumaturgic power, and racist view of psychoanalysis as a 'Jewish psychology', were, at the very least, grist to the Nazi propaganda mill.

Freud clung to the prevalent belief that the spread of Nazism would be confined by France and the League of Nations. However, by 1937 this was impossible to sustain and he became convinced that a German invasion of Austria was inevitable, remarking despondently, 'My only hope is that I shall not live to see it.'[4] He had passed his eightieth year and, looking back on his accomplishments, wrote to the novelist, Stefan Zweig, 'My work lies behind me, as you say. No one can predict how later epochs will assess it. I myself am not so sure; doubt can never be divorced from research, and I have assuredly not dug up more than a fragment of truth.'[5]

In fact, the judgement of psychoanalysis has been remarkably difficult for history to make. A century of controversy has done little to resolve the key issues concerning its nature and value. The only thing upon which critics seem to agree is the profundity of its intellectual influence in our times.

Notwithstanding the personal invective levelled at Freud and his followers, exemplified by the scurrilous Viennese satirist Karl Kraus – 'If mankind, with all its repulsive faults, is an organism, then the psychoanalyst is its excrement'[6] – two important questions echo down the years. What is its scientific status? What is its therapeutic usefulness?

Philosophers of science, psychiatrists and psychoanalysts themselves have been divided in their opinions. As long ago as 1910, Alfred Hoche, Professor of Psychiatry at Freiburg, asserted in an extravagant diatribe entitled 'A Psychical Epidemic among Doctors' that psychoanalysis did not deal in facts capable of being tested scientifically, but with articles of faith. It was a religious sect, he asserted, with Freud as its high priest. In similar vein, speaking fifteen years later, the American psychologist J. McKeen Cattell dismissed psychoanalysis as 'not so much a question of science as a matter of taste, Dr Freud being an artist who lives in the fairyland of dreams among the ogres of perverted sex'.[7]

Religion, myth and science all describe, explain and claim to predict events. But whereas, according to the philosopher Karl Popper, the former are typically eternal and incorrigible, it is characteristic of scientific theories to be provisional and open to correction by new evidence. If the role of religion and myth is to provide an authoritative (culturally acceptable) logic that accommodates the mysteries of life, the role of science is to frame theories which have the potential to be undermined by experience.

Some contemporary critics follow Hoche and Cattell, arguing that psychoanalysis fails to specify what would count as disconfirming evidence. Others point to the modifications forced on Freud by clinical observation and assert that the complex interplay between fact and theory is (only) open to investigation by anyone willing to follow his method. A third group believes that the theories can be stated in terms which render them publicly testable (by non-analysts), but research in this genre has produced equivocal results.

Although psychoanalytic practice has grown steadily more sensitive over the years, the body of psychoanalytic knowledge has not expanded in the manner of a natural science. Its empirical bearing has had to be rediscovered by every practitioner, through personal experience. And its application to individual cases in the consulting room has the character of a craft, rather than a technology.

Many analysts now consider Havelock Ellis, the great Victorian sexologist, to have been correct in regarding their work as an art, though such a view was unwelcome to Freud – 'the most refined and amiable form of resistance, calling me a great artist in order to injure the validity of our scientific claims'.[8] However, the value of psychoanalysis, creating as it does a dialogue of unparalleled intimacy, may lie more in its capacity to respond to distinctively individual human needs than in the application of scientific generalisations. For this reason, while personal anecdotes and professional case studies have convinced many of its efficacy, systematic assessment using standardised outcome measures and statistically controlled comparison groups has seemed alien to its nature. Nonetheless, what research there is tends to confirm psychoanalytic therapies as beneficial.[9]

Yet Freud's character has been impeached and his work decried, as violently after death as it was in life. His astonishing capacity to provoke controversy is unabated. In December 1995, under the headline 'Freud May Be Dead But His Critics Still Kick', the *New York Times* reported the postponement by the Library of Congress of a major exhibition on Freud, following protests by scholars. Museums, it said, were becoming increasingly politicised. Prevailing anti-Freudian orthodoxy appeared to be fast developing into a form of political correctness reminiscent of McCarthyism.

In many respects psychoanalysis has been a victim of its own success. Every psychoanalytic truth has become a cliché, something we have always known; every mistaken inference a 'news item', taken to discredit the whole. It has always been the whipping boy for aspects of human nature it had the temerity to expose. Freud did not invent the unconscious, sexual abuse, the fallibility of memory or the symbolic capacity of the imagination, but he introduced them to the public.

His rich legacy has stimulated philosophical debate and psychological enquiry for a hundred years. It has informed the development of social science, literary criticism and cultural analysis, shaped our attitudes towards education, institutional care and child-rearing, and left us with a sophisticated therapeutic method, uniquely attuned to the complexity of the human mind.

NOTES

CHAPTER ONE

1. Cited in P. Gay, *Freud: A Life for Our Time* (1988), p. 628.
2. E. Jones, *The Life and Work of Sigmund Freud* (1962), edited and abridged by L. Trilling and S. Marcus, p. 636.
3. R. McCully, 'Remarks on the Last Contact between Freud and Jung', *Quadrant*, 20 (1987), pp. 73–4, cited in F. McLynn, *Carl Gustav Jung* (1996), p. 417.
4. Gay, *Freud*, p. 631.
5. B. Wasserstein, *Britain and the Jews of Europe 1939–1945* (1979), p. 11.
6. Jones, *Freud*, p. 655.
7. Ibid, p. 657.
8. W.H. Auden, 'In Memory of Sigmund Freud', in *Collected Shorter Poems 1927–1957* (1966), p. 168.

CHAPTER TWO

1. S. Freud, *The Interpretation of Dreams* (1900, footnote added 1911), SE5, p. 398.
2. S. Freud, 'Screen Memories' (1899), SE3, p. 301.
3. Ibid, p. 311.
4. Freud, *Interpretation of Dreams*, SE4, p. 197.
5. Ibid, p. 193.

CHAPTER THREE

1. Letter from Freud to Martha Bernays, 2 June 1884, cited in Jones, *Freud*, p. 95.
2. S. Freud, 'Autobiographical Study' (1925), SE20, p. 10.
3. Letter from Freud to Bernays, 2 June 1884.
4. See A. Schacter (ed.), *Treatment Aspects of Drug Dependence* (1978), CRC Press, Florida.

5. H. Decker, *Freud in Germany: Revolution and Reaction in Science, 1893–1907* (1977), International Universities Press, p. 77.

6. See C. Mace and M. Trimble, 'Ten Year Prognosis of Conversion Disorder', *British Journal of Psychiatry* (1996), pp. 282–8.

7. S. Freud, 'Preface and Footnotes to the Translation of Charcot's Tuesday Lectures', SE1, p. 139.

CHAPTER FOUR

1. S. Freud, 'The Psychotherapy of Hysteria' in *Studies on Hysteria* (1893), SE2, p. 265.

2. Jones, *Freud*, p. 145.

3. Ibid, p. 149.

4. M. Freud, *Sigmund Freud: Man and Father* (1983), p. 27.

5. Jones, *Freud*, p. 203.

6. Quoted in Gay, *Freud*, p. 67.

7. S. Freud, 'On the Psychical Mechanism of Hysterical Phenomena: Preliminary Communication' (1893), SE2, p. 7.

CHAPTER FIVE

1. S. Freud, *The Interpretation of Dreams* (1900), translated by A. Brill, p. 447.

2. A. Hirshmüller, *Physiologie und Psychoanalyse in Lebern und Werk: Josef Breuers* (1978), p. 324, cited in P. Swales, 'Freud, Fliess and Fratricide: The Role of Fliess in Freud's Conception of Paranoia', in *Sigmund Freud: Critical Assessments* (1989), p. 305.

3. Letter, 12 December 1897; see Masson, p. 285.

4. J. Masson, *The Assault on Truth: Freud's Suppression of the Seduction Theory* (1985).

5. Letter, 30 July 1898, in *The Complete Letters of Sigmund Freud and Wilhelm Fliess, 1887–1904*, translated and edited by J. Masson (1985), p. 320.

6. Jones, *Freud*, p. 258.

7. H. Ellenberger, *The Discovery of the Unconscious* (1994), p. 447.

8. Masson, *Letters*, p. 422.

9. Swales, *Fliess*, p. 311.

10. Masson, *Letters*, p. 264.

11. Freud, *Dreams*, p. 262.

12. Masson, *The Assault*.

CHAPTER SIX

1. Jones, *Freud*, p. 299.

2. Masson, *Letters*, p. 417.

3. Freud, *Dreams*, SE5, p. 608.

4. Freud, *Dreams*, translated by Brill, p. 183.

5. Ibid, p. 165.

6. Masson, *Letters*, p. 457.

CHAPTER SEVEN

1. Letter to Karl Abraham, 3 May 1908, in *A Psycho-analytic Dialogue: The Letters of Sigmund Freud and Karl Abraham 1907–1926*, H. Abraham and E. Freud (eds), 1965, p. 34.

2. S. Freud, *The Psychopathology of Everyday Life*, 1901, SE6; S. Freud, *Jokes and their Relation to the Unconscious*, 1905, SE8.

3. Freud, SE8.

4. Jones, *Freud*, p. 404.

5. Letter from Jung to Freud, 21 June 1909, cited in McLynn, *Jung*.

6. Letter, December 1910, cited in Gay, *Freud*, p. 201.

7. Freud, *On the History of the Psycho-Analytic Movement*, SE14, p. 51.

8. W. McGuire (ed.), *The Freud–Jung Letters*, 1974, pp. 539, 540.

CHAPTER EIGHT

1. S. Freud, *Thoughts for the Times on War and Death*, 1915, SE14, p. 299.

2. Jones, *Freud*, p. 433.

3. Freud, *Dreams*, p. 558.

4. Freud, *Dreams*, SE5, p. 560.

5. Freud, *Dreams*, Ibid.

6. Jones, *Freud*, p. 441.

7. Gay, *Freud*, p. 441.

Notes

CHAPTER NINE

1. Jones, *Freud*, p. 553.
2. Masson, *Letters*, p. 132.
3. Freud, *Beyond the Pleasure Principle*, SE18, p. 38.
4. Jones, *Freud*, p. 547.
5. Freud, *New Introductory Lectures* (1933), SE22, p. 80.
6. Jones, *Freud*, p. 523.
7. M. Stanton, *Sándor Ferenczi* (1990), p. 48.
8. Jones, *Freud*, p. 600.
9. W. Shakespeare, *The Merchant of Venice*, II, 9, 39.

CHAPTER TEN

1. S. Freud, *Analysis Terminable and Interminable*, SE23, p. 229.
2. Gay, *Freud*, p. 491.
3. Ibid.
4. Jones, *Freud*, p. 633.
5. Ibid, p. 634.
6. T. Szasz, *Anti-Freud: Karl Kraus's Criticism of Psychoanalysis and Psychiatry* (1990), p. 115.
7. Gay, *Freud*, p. 493.
8. Jones, *Freud*, p. 493.
9. S. Fisher and R. Greenberg, *Freud Scientifically Reappraised* (1996), p. 260.

BIBLIOGRAPHY

Publishers' location is London, unless otherwise stated.

FREUD'S WORK

Strachey, James (ed.), *Standard Edition of the Complete Psychological Works of Sigmund Freud* (24 vols), Hogarth Press, 1953–74

The Penguin Freud Library (15 vols), Pelican, 1973–86

FREUD'S LIFE

Gay, P., *Freud: A Life for Our Time*, Macmillan, 1995

Jones, E., *The Life and Work of Sigmund Freud* (3 vols), Hogarth Press, 1957, edited and abridged by L. Trilling and S. Marcus, Pelican, 1964

Molnar, M., 'Sigmund Freud (1856–1939): Life and Work', *Journal of Medical Biography,* 4, 1996, 236–43

CITED IN TEXT

Abraham, H. and Freud, E. (eds), *A Psychoanalytic Dialogue: The Letters of Sigmund Freud and Karl Abraham 1907–1926*, Hogarth Press, 1965

Auden, W.H., *Collected Shorter Poems 1927–1957*, Faber, 1966

Decker, H., *Freud in Germany: Revolution and Reaction in Science, 1893–1907*, New York, International Universities Press, 1977

Bibliography

Ellenberger, H., *The Discovery of the Unconscious: The History and Evolution of Dynamic Psychiatry*, Fontana Press, 1994

Fisher, S. and Greenberg, R., *Freud Scientifically Reappraised*, New York, Wiley, 1996

Freud, M., *Sigmund Freud: Man and Father*, Jason Aronson, 1983

Mace, C. and Trimble, M., 'Ten-year Prognosis of Conversion Disorder', *British Journal of Psychiatry,* 169, 1996, 282–8

Masson, J., *The Assault on Truth: Freud's Suppression of the Seduction Theory*, Penguin, 1985

—— (ed.), *The Complete Letters of Sigmund Freud to Wilhelm Fliess, 1887–1904*, Harvard University Press, 1985

McGuire, W., *The Freud–Jung Letters: The Correspondence between Sigmund Freud and C.G. Jung,* Penguin, 1991

McLynn, F., *Carl Gustav Jung*, Transworld, 1996

Schacter, A. (ed.), *Treatment Aspects of Drug Dependence*, Florida, CRC Press, 1978

Spurling, L. (ed.), *Sigmund Freud: Critical Assessments* (4 vols), Routledge, 1989

Stanton, M., *Sándor Ferenczi: Reconsidering Active Intervention*, Free Association Books, 1990

Swales, P., 'Freud, Fliess, and Fratricide: The role of Fliess in Freud's conception of paranoia', in Spurling, *Sigmund Freud*, 1989

Szasz, T., *Anti-Freud: Karl Kraus's Criticism of Psychoanalysis and Psychiatry*, New York, Wiley, 1996

Wasserstein, B., *Britain and the Jews of Europe 1939–1945*, Oxford University Press, 1979

FURTHER READING

Farrel, B. (ed.), *Philosophy and Psychoanalysis*, Macmillan, 1994

Kline, P., *Psychology and Freudian Theory: An Introduction*, Methuen, 1984

Macmillan, M., *Freud Evaluated: The Completed Arc*, New York, MIT Press, 1997

Paul, R., *Moses and Civilisation: The Meaning behind Freud's Myth*, Yale University Press, 1996

Rieff, P., *Freud: The Mind of the Moralist*, Methuen, 1965

Robert, M., *From Oedipus to Moses: Freud's Jewish Identity*, Routledge and Kegan Paul/Littman Library, 1974

Robinson, P., *Freud and his Critics*, Berkeley, University of California Press, 1993

Rudnytsky, P., *Freud and Oedipus*, Guildford, Columbia University Press, 1987

Storr, A., *Freud*, Oxford University Press, 1989

Sulloway, F., *Freud, Biologist of the Mind*, Fontana, 1980

Welsh, A., *Freud's Wishful Dream Book*, Chichester, Princeton University Press, 1994

Wistrich, R., *The Jews of Vienna in the Age of Franz Joseph*, Oxford University Press/Littman Library, 1990

POCKET BIOGRAPHIES

This series looks at the lives of those who have played a significant part in our history – from musicians to explorers, from scientists to entertainers, from writers to philosophers, from politicians to monarchs throughout the world. Concise and highly readable, with black and white plates, chronology and bibliography, these books will appeal to students and general readers alike.

Available

Beethoven
Anne Pimlott Baker

Mao Zedong
Delia Davin

Scott of the Antarctic
Michael De-la-Noy

Alexander the Great
E.E. Rice

Marilyn Monroe
Sheridan Morley and
Ruth Leon

Rasputin
Harold Shukman

Jane Austen
Helen Lefroy

POCKET BIOGRAPHIES

Forthcoming

Marie and Pierre Curie
John Senior

Ellen Terry
Moira Shearer

David Livingstone
Christine Nicholls

Margot Fonteyn
Alistair Macauley

Winston Churchill
Robert Blake

Abraham Lincoln
H.G. Pitt

Charles Dickens
Catherine Peters

Enid Blyton
George Greenfield